Joseph Banvard

Soldiers and Patriots of the American Revolution

Joseph Banvard

Soldiers and Patriots of the American Revolution

ISBN/EAN: 9783337307547

Printed in Europe, USA, Canada, Australia, Japan

Cover: Foto ©ninafisch / pixelio.de

More available books at **www.hansebooks.com**

Faneuil Hall, Boston. Page 33.

PIONEERS
OF THE
NEW WORLD.
BY
JOSEPH BANVARD

4 Vols.

Plymouth and the Pilgrims.
Southern Explorers and Colonists.
Pioneers of Maryland.
Soldiers and Patriots of the Revolution.

SOLDIERS AND PATRIOTS

OF THE

AMERICAN REVOLUTION.

BY
JOSEPH BANVARD, D. D.

Boston:
Published by D. Lothrop & Co.
Dover, N.H.: G. T. Day & Co.

Copyright, 1876, by D. LOTHROP & CO.

CONTENTS.

CHAPTER I.
FAREWELL TO THE RED-COATS	7

CHAPTER II.
THE BOSTON MASSACRE	11

CHAPTER III.
A GLORIOUS BONFIRE	20

CHAPTER IV.
YANKEE INDIANS	30

CHAPTER V.
LEXINGTON AND CONCORD	42

CHAPTER VI.
THE GREEN MOUNTAIN BOYS	59

CHAPTER VII.
BUNKER HILL	65

CHAPTER VIII.
THE SIEGE OF BOSTON	84

CHAPTER IX.
THE UNEXPECTED GUEST. . . . 95

CHAPTER X.
MAC'S ESCAPE 108

CHAPTER XI.
HIDE-AND-SEEK WITH THE RED-SKINS . 119

CHAPTER XII.
KING'S MOUNTAIN 131

CHAPTER XIII.
MAD ANTONY 140

CHAPTER XIV.
WASHINGTON'S STRATAGEM . . . 148

CHAPTER XV.
AN ARMY CAUGHT NAPPING . . . 157

CHAPTER XVI.
THE BOLD MANŒUVRE 171

CHAPTER XVII.
RECAPTURE OF THE "GENERAL MONK" . 183

CHAPTER XVIII.
THE WYOMING MASSACRE. . . . 192

CHAPTER XIX.
YORKTOWN DAY 205

CHAPTER XX.
A GLIMPSE OF OLD '77 217

CHAPTER XXI.
THE CAPTURE OF GENERAL BURGOYNE . 227

CHAPTER XXII.
THE BRAVE BRITISH WIFE . . . 236

CHAPTER XXIII.
THE BATTLE OF BENNINGTON . . . 239

CHAPTER XXIV.
WASHINGTON'S FAREWELL . . . 245

CHAPTER XXV.
COL. BRATTON'S WIFE 251

CHAPTER XXVI.
THE CONCEALED GUARD 262

CHAPTER XXVII.
DEBORAH SAMSON, THE GIRL SOLDIER . 273

CHAPTER XXVIII.
SOLDIERS' YARNS 284

SOLDIERS AND PATRIOTS

OF THE REVOLUTION.

CHAPTER I.

FAREWELL TO THE RED-COATS.

"Hurrah! hurrah! the twenty-fifth of November, a day never to be forgotten — a day next to the Fourth of July — Hurrah! Honor to George Washington! Thanks to the Continental army! Glory to God!"

Such was the joyous exclamation of an old revolutionary veteran, as he entered the dooryard of his little cottage, on Broadway, New

York, near where the hospital now stands. With his cane, his wooden leg, and his stout lungs, he created quite a furor among the little folks who were playing in the neighborhood, and many of them followed him to his door. "Hurrah" continued the old man, "the war is over; peace is declared, and the last red-coat is drummed out of the country. I tell you it did my old eyes good to see the Britishers leave the wharf this morning" and the lips of the veteran trembled and the tears coursed down his wrinkled cheeks.

"I guess Uncle Tim loves to see sogers about as well as we do" said a roguish-looking urchin.

"Aye, aye, Bobby, there's no handsomer sight on the broad earth than regiments of the enemy in full retreat. Boys," continued the lame warrior, to the group of children around him, "if you had been on the battle-field where I have been, with the wounded, the dying, and the dead all around you, and these same red-coats shooting down your friends, and fighting to get your liberty away, you would know just how I feel to see them beaten and driven home. As the last company of 'em left our shores this morning I thought over the whole war; I thought of all the wretchedness they had caused us, the number they had slain, and of the multitudes they have left behind them, mutilated like myself. I thought of the contrast between *their* condition when they landed, and their condition now, and when I realized that all this terrible work was ended; that we had conquered the British and broken the tyrant yoke, and secured a glorious independence, my heart leaped, and I seemed as young as you. Why, I almost fancied I had the leg I lost at Monmouth back again whole and sound and could feel the blood throb through it as warm as ever!"

"Are these the same sogers," asked a little light-headed, blue-eyed boy, named Tommy Brown, "are these the same sogers I read about that shot down the people in the streets of Boston?"

"They belong to the same army," replied the veteran, dropping into his great high-backed, rush-bottomed chair. Uncle Tim always sat in this chair when he read the papers, or talked with the boys.

"That Boston massacre was a most monstrous piece of wickedness. I lived in Boston at the time, and I remember all about it"

"Do tell it to us, Uncle" cried several voices at once. "You know we always love to hear your stories."

"You don't like to hear them any better than I love to tell them," said Uncle Tim.

CHAPTER II.

THE BOSTON MASSACRE.

"You see, boys, the Boston Massacre was not exactly a revolutionary event, as it occurred on the fifth day of March, 1770, a little more than six years before the Declaration of Independence, and before the war of the Revolution had commenced. Still it was one of the things that helped bring it on. The British government sent two regiments of soldiers to Boston, to frighten the discontented inhabitants, and keep them quiet and obedient. They landed on Sunday with all the array of war, marched with flag and fife and drum through the streets, and took up their quarters in the town. Boston saw itself turned into an oppressor's garrison. The presence of those troops was a shame and an irritation to every patriotic citizen."

"And what made them shoot the people?" asked the little blue-eyed boy.

"Well, Tommy, I am coming to that," said Uncle Tim. "On the 22d of February several boys went through the streets of Boston carrying pictures of certain merchants who were known to be importers of English goods, and who, of course, were unpopular. They did this in order to ridicule the merchants, and to cast odium upon their conduct; for the British government had so oppressed the people by the Stamp Act, as it was called, that American patriots had agreed to buy and use no more English goods. I saw these pictures, or effigies, and could not help laughing at them. While these boys were having their sport in the streets, they were met by a royalist — that is, one who took sides with the King of England. This royalist was a spy upon the people, and was accustomed to give information against them to the government officers.

"At the same moment I noticed a countryman coming down the street. The royalist tried to induce this man to destroy these pictures which the boys were carrying. He wisely declined.

"The royalist then made the attempt himself. The boys resisted. An altercation ensued; and a crowd soon collected. Some sympathized with the boys, and encouraged them. This made the royalist more angry, and he began to pour out his abuse upon the citizens,—accusing some of them of perjury, and threatening to have them prosecuted. They however regarded these threats as too insignificant for notice.

"But the boys who had the pictures, irritated at the man's interference, followed him to his home, retaliating as best they could by calling after him with reproaches and noisy ridicule.

"As soon as the man had entered his dwelling, he seized a gun and appeared at a window with it in his hands, thinking to terrify the boys. But this only aggravated them the more, and they began to throw snow-balls and stones.

"The incensed royalist then levelled his musket through the window, and fired. It was a fatal shot. One of the boys fell dead in the street. This created a great excitement among the people.

"An immense multitude attended the funeral of the poor boy and followed his body to the grave-yard. They considered him a youthful *martyr* to the cause of liberty."

"How did the soldiers behave after that?" asked Tommy Brown.

"After that, when they strolled through the town, they usually carried large clubs with them. They knew how heartily the people disliked the army, and they were always ready to pick a quarrel.

"On the 2d of March they insulted some rope-makers. This provoked a fight, in which a number on both sides were wounded. These assaults were repeated upon the rope-walk with new aggravations and greater excitement every time. The indignation of the citizens against the redcoats increased day by day.

"Finally, on the evening of March 5th, a party of seven or eight armed soldiers, under the command of Captain Preston, were seen in King Street in front of the custom-house.

"A good many people were already assembled there, some from curiosity, and others because they expected another fight with the soldiers, and were resolved to take part in it.

"On these the British soldiers fired, and eleven of the crowd fell! Oh, it was a horrid sight to see the citizens of Boston shot down in cold blood!" And the old man shuddered, and paused in his story, as the scene passed again before his mind.

"Did all the soldiers fire together?" asked little Tommy.

"No, one gun was fired first, but that did no injury. Then two reports were heard, and immediately two persons in the crowd fell dead."

"Oh, I am glad I was not there!" cried Tommy.

"Keep still," said one of the boys, "Uncle Tim hasn't got through yet."

"Who were the two that were killed?"

"One of them," replied Uncle Tim, "was Samuel Gray, a rope-maker, and the other was a mulatto. The excitement was furious now, and between the soldiers and citizens the long hatred flamed into deadly rage. Three or four more guns were fired, and two other men fell wounded. Then five shots followed, three of them from the custom-house windows, wounding several more. Thus the firing continued until eleven persons were shot. But as if murdering our patriots with bullets were not barbarity enough, one of the cowardly red-coats ran to Mr. Gray as he lay dead, and plunged a bayonet into his head, scattering his brains upon the pavement! My blood boils even now, as I remember that shocking deed!

"The affair made a terrible sensation, not only

in Massachusetts, but through all the colonies. It occurred on Monday, and on Thursday the funeral of the slaughtered citizens took place.

"It was a very solemn time. The stores were closed, and the tolling bells of Boston and the neighboring towns filled the air with mournful music. The procession met in King Street, near the scene of the massacre. The funeral then passed on to the burying-ground, where the martyrs were all deposited in one vault. *

"You can hardly understand, boys, how intense was the horror and wrath awakened throughout the colonies, when once the enemy had shed patriot blood. These outrages deepened our opposition against British oppression, and made war inevitable. They served also to increase the sympathy and union of the colonies with each other, so that they could plan together, and arm themselves as one against the common foe."

* King Street is now called State Street. The place of the massacre was in State Street, just below the old State House, and near the corner of Wilson's Lane. The Custom-House was on the corner of Wilson's Lane and State Street, where the Merchant's Bank now stands. The soldiers stood immediately in front of this when they fired.

"I guess they didn't forget those murders very soon," said Tommy Brown.

"No indeed," replied Uncle Tim. "The Anniversary of the massacre was celebrated publicly every year. And on these occasions our most eloquent orators addressed the people, and stirred them up to be watchful, and, when the time came, to fight for their liberties.

"So the spirit of resistance in the people was kept alive, and their patriotism took fire at the slightest alarm. This was shown when they threw the tea over-board in Boston Harbor, and afterwards, when they faced the Red-Coats at Lexington, and on Bunker-Hill."

"What was done with the soldiers who committed the murders?" asked one of the boys.

"They were brought to trial," said Uncle Tim. "Captain Preston, who commanded the company, and six of the men, were acquitted. Two others were found guilty of manslaughter."

It was now near sunset, and the old man's supper was ready. "Come boys," said he, as he rose up from his great chair, and stood very straight, "Let's give three cheers for Washington and Independence!"

Instantly the whole circle of little patriots shouted at the top of their lungs "Hurra! Hurra! Hurra!"

And then they separated for the night.

CHAPTER III.

A GLORIOUS BONFIRE.

"POMP, you're a hero!" shouted a group of young men on the Park in the city of New York, who were surrounding a poor colored man known as Pompey Ducklegs.

"Capital, Pomp! You're a hero, Pomp! tell us some more of your adventures."

Pompey was a great favorite with the citizens. His peculiar cognomen of Ducklegs was given him because he had lost the lower part of both his legs, which compelled him to waddle along, at a slow pace, upon his knees. He was a man of more than ordinary intelligence and wit, and as he had been in a number of engagements in the war, his descriptions of scenes he had witnessed were always interesting to the people. Whenever he chose to talk he never wanted for listeners.

"When I was took from de West Injy's, whar de kidnappers leff me," said Pompey, "I come to Rhode Island, an' stayed dar till de war broke out. I was dar when de ole Gaspee was burnt, an' I had a hand in it."

"Good. You shared in the glory, did you?" asked one of the crowd.

"You're right," said Pomp. "An' dar was glory 'nuff in de high ole bonfire dat ship made. De great blazes went squirmin' up her riggin' like snakes; an' when de masts fell thunderin' down alongside dey made a 'lumination roun' de whole harbor, tree or fo' miles. You'd a tought de lass day was come."

"Tell us how you captured her, Pompey."

"Yes, give us the whole story," said several voices.

Pomp saw his audience was interested, and a grin of satisfaction gleamed in his black face.

"I lived in Providence dem times," he went on, "an a British schooner was lyin' in de bay, to keep a look-out on Yankee boats, so dey shouldn't smuggle goods ashore — an' 'tween you an' I, boys, I used t' be up to a little smugglin' myseff, once 'n a while, yah, yah!"

"Wal, you see, de cap'n o' dat schooner was a bumptious ole buck, an' he wanted all de vessels comin' in to Providence to lower dere flags an' s'lute him when dey pas' by."

"How did the Yankees like that?"

"Oh, it made 'em mad, an' some on 'em *wouldn't do it.*"

"What happened then?"

"Why den," answered Pompey, "de British cap'n would bang a gun at 'em, an' chase em' way into port. I tell you 'twas crank fun to see de racin' such times. Jolly! how de 'people used to run down to shore, and on de way, to look! An' wen a Yankee beat de ole Britisher, how de boys used to swing hats and holler!"

"But the Gaspee, the Gaspee? what of her?" demanded an impatient listener.

"Wal, ye see when de Gaspee lay dar watchin', a Providence packet come in. Her cap'n was a high-strung fellow, an' he wouldn't take off his cap and make a bow to no British schooner nowhar. So he kep his flag a flyin', an' sailed on. De big British cap'n felt insulted, and fired off a gun to bring him to. Yah, yah you bet he nebber stopped for dat. He didn't min' nothin' 'bout it, but kep' right on, jes' as if dey hadn't been nobody dar. Ole Britisher got hoppin' mad now, so he up anchor, an' took arter dat Yankee, full sail.

"But Yank knew dem waters better'n he did; so when he seed de red-flag schooner chasin', he tought he'd manage it so t' fetch him aground. 'Twas high tide, ye see, an' all de shoals and wuss places was under water out o' sight. Tell ye, boys, 'twas play to see dat packet steer up, an' rub close in shore, wid de Britisher right in her wake! We all knew, well 'nuff, what was comin'. In a little while — smack! dar stood ole schooner still as a post, wid her sails all hoisted, stock in de mud — an' de big cap'n rippin' an' tearin' to split hisself. Ki, how tickled 'Mericans were! De packet come in all safe, with flag apeak, an' when our Yankee cap'n came ashore, how he and de wharf folks did laaf! Wal, 'twasn't long 'fore eberybody knew de British spy was aground. Some darin' feller said, 'Come, let's go *burn her!*' Others was 'fraid, an' said, 'No, no! we'll have a whole English fleet upon us. 'Den we'll *burn dem too!*' says one.

"So de matter was talked ober till de people got all in a fume 'bout it; an' finally, a lot on em 'greed to go. Dar was Massa Brown, a rich merchant, an' Cap'n Whipple, dat ebery body knowed and 'spected, an' dem two men was to take de lead. Cap'n Whipple knowed me, for I'd sailed wid him as cook seberal times. 'Pomp,' says he to me, 'would you like to go?' (You see dey didn't call me Pompey Ducklegs, 'cause I hadn't lost my legs.) 'Aye, aye, sir,' says I. 'Be on hand at twelve o'clock to-night,' says he. An' you bet I was dar, prompt and airly. Dey fixed upon a place to meet, an' at midnight a good many men got together on shore, all armed with swords and muskets. We had a power o' fixin' and waitin' to do, but, finally, 'bout one or two o'clock, we all got off in some whale boats. We rowed mighty cautious, an' whispered when we had to say anything. Bimeby we come close to de schooner, but we didn't see nor hear nobody. I s'pose de sentry was asleep. An' fact, boys, we all clim' up de sides o' dat vessel, an' *got aboard*, 'fore de British knowed anything 'bout it. When de cap'n waked up an' found out what was goin' on, he showed fight; but one on us pricked him wid a sword, an' he concluded to keep still. De sailors all see it was no use, an' dey gin up, too. Jolly! we'd captured an English man-o'-war, an' ossifers an' crew — an' never fired a gun! Dat was de one time I felt like I wanted to *brag*, boys."

"Hurra for you, Pompey!" said several of the young men.

"Well, what did you do after you got possession?"

"Why, part on us took de prisoners an' de booty ashore, an' part on us stayed aboard. I was in de boat wid de ossifers, and arter we'd rowed a good ways, I seed some lights moving about on de deck, and pretty soon I seed a blaze. Fus' it was a little one, but it growed bigger mighty fas'. 'Fire, fire!' hollered one of our men. De cap'n o' de Gaspee looked roun' an' seed his vessel dar all in a flame. Oh, how he did rave, an' cuss de Yankees! De fire crep' up an up, an' roun' an' roun', till it catched the upper cross-trees, an' wrapped every sail an' rope, an' shot over the sky-pole, an lit out on de water as bright as moonshine; only 'twas red, red eberywhere.

"De sky was all red, an' de sea was all red,

an' de lan' was all red. You nebber seed a splendider 'lumination. People come down sho' from miles off to look at dat bonfire, and dey stood in big crowds all along. An' de fire kep' burnin' an' burnin', till it tetched the powder-mag'zine, an' den all went off, whang! wid a noise that seemed like it shook de worl'. One minute all heaben an' earth was streamin' light wi' sparks an fire-bran's, an de nex' minute it went out and leff us in de blackest darkness I ebber know'd. Nobody hollered den. It was too awful. But dar was no more Gaspee — dar, nor anywhere."

"What happened the next day, when the authorities learned about it?"

"Wall, I'll tell ye," said Pomp, putting on a mysterious look. "I'll tell ye what happened to me. I los' *five hunderd poun's* by dat affair."

"Why, Pompey, you don't mean it!"

"Yes, sah, *five hund'd poun's*. Enuff to made a rich man o' me. I los' it, an' I didn't cry about it, needur."

"That was too bad!" said several voices.

"No it warn't," said Pomp; "an if it had been five times more I wouldn't a' cared."

"Now, Pomp, you're joking. Explain yourself," said his young audience.

"Why, you see, boys," answered the old negro, breaking into a grin, "de gubment offered a reward o' five hund'd poun's to anybody as 'ud tell who took an' burnt de Gaspee, or a single name on 'em, an' if him as told was one in de scrape hisself, he should receive bofe de money an, a pardon besides. Now I knowed a good many as was in dat party, an' if I'd tole on 'em, I'd a been a rich man. I los' dat money, young gemmen, 'cause why? I had a padlock on my mouf. I wouldn't a tole for five thousan' poun'. You hear?"

"That's just like you, Pomp. You're a hero to the backbone. Did any one else ever get the reward?"

"No, sah. Dar warn't one o' dat comp'ny mean enuff, an' nobody else knowed. Five hundred poun's couldn't buy a man of us. But laws! didn't de affair make a big 'citement all roun' dar! Eberybody was wond'rin'. Some said de king would send ober an army, an' whip us rite off. But de res' said, 'Let 'em come, an' we'll show you what Yankees can do ebery time.' Now, young gemmen, if ye'll help a poor, lame niggah to a few pennies, he'll be berry t'ankful."

He held up his old, torn hat, and received quite a generous contribution from his audience, who had been immensely entertained both by his narrative, and by his way of telling it. They then dispersed, leaving Pomp to waddle home on his duck legs, as best he could.

CHAPTER IV.

YANKEE INDIANS.

ONE pleasant Saturday afternoon Uncle Tim was sitting in his accustomed place in front of his house, when Tommy Brown and his friend Bobby were seen slowly approaching him, looking very earnestly upon a small piece of paper which they held between them, and at the same time engaged in earnest conversation.

"What have you there, my boys," said the old soldier, "that interests you so much?"

"It's a picture of the Boston Tea Party,' answered Tommy.

"The Boston Tea Party, hey? ha! ha! ha! A good subject, my boys, a good subject for a picture; let me see if I should know it," said he, reaching out his hand.

"Oh, yes," said he, as he looked at it, "that's it — that'll do very well. There they are, ships, stores, Indians, spectators and all. There they are. I tell you what, boys, that was a big thing, and it required pluck to manage it."

"Were you there?" asked little Bobby.

"Yes, indeed, I guess I was," replied the old man, "and I learnt one thing that night."

"What was that?" inquired Tommy.

"I learnt how to make Indians. Yes, how to make Indians out of Yankees. And if you won't tell, boys, I'll let you into a secret," continued the old man, lowering his voice almost to a whisper, "*I was one of them.*"

"What," said Tommy, "one of these Indians?"

"Yes, I was a Mohawk Indian that night; and for more than two hours I stirred British tea there, with a tomahawk for a tea-spoon.

We made it hot, too. Oh, but that was a lively party!"

"What was it all about, Uncle Tim?" asked little Bobby.

"What was it all about? Why, boy, the King of England sent over here a law that no tea should be landed in America unless we paid a tax of three pence a pound on it. That law was made by the British Parliament three thousand miles from here, and, what is more, they wouldn't allow any of us colonists to have a place in that Parliament, to represent the country and vote for our rights.

"Well, the Americans thought that was high-handed tyranny. 'Let us send men of our own to Parliament to represent us, and speak for us,' said we. 'No,' said they, ' we don't want American representatives here. We will make laws for you to suit ourselves, and you must submit.' And so they passed this law about the tea. It made us very indignant, you may guess. Public meetings were held all over the country, and spirited speeches kindled up the excitement to fever heat. The people were appealed to by their love of country and their love of liberty, to resist the execution of this unjust law. England had no right to tax us without our consent, no matter whether it was three pence or a hundred pence, and we did not mean to let the old government begin to make slaves of us, in that way or in any other way.

"During the excitement two vessels, laden with tea, arrived at Boston. And now the struggle commenced in earnest. A large public meeting was called in Faneuil Hall, of the inhabitants of Boston and of the surrounding towns, and then the patriots discussed the matter, and took measures to prevent the landing of the tea. The merchants, to whom the tea had been sent, were requested not to receive it. The captains who brought it over were told to take it back. But the Governor of the colony would not let them go. Some of the merchants were willing to have it landed, and when the people learned this, they were so indignant that they went in crowds, and surrounded the dwellings of these merchants, and frightened them so that they fled for safety to Fort William, on one of the islands in Boston Harbor. It was then proposed to the citizens that the tea be landed and placed in some strong store-house for safe keeping.

"But the inhabitants would not listen to this. They were determined that no tea should come *into the country* until the tax on it was removed. The Governor at the same time was determined that the tea should not be taken back to England nor carried away from Boston. As it was a possible thing for the tea to be landed privately, the citizens appointed a guard to watch the vessels night and day, so that their cargoes could not be discharged without its being known.

"Matters were rapidly coming to a crisis, and on the 14th of December, 1773, a large 'Town Meeting' was held in Faneuil Hall, to take final and decisive action.

"But the leading citizens, still desirous of making some orderly terms with Governor Hutchinson, were not quite ready to go to extremes, and this meeting was adjourned two days. The 16th of December came, the memorable Thursday, and the people assembled, not in Faneuil Hall, but in the Old South church. The great orators spoke there, and their words roused every patriot to the last energy of resolution.

"Josiah Quincy, Jr., made a speech at that meeting that thrilled every hearer, and nerved the weakest patriot to a grand resistance. He told them they must do something now, and not end it all in talk, for they were approaching the most terrible and trying struggle the country had ever seen. The people believed it, and voted to stand by their first determination not to let the tea be landed. They then sent a deputation to the Governor to get his permission for the ships to depart. The Governor obstinately refused. When the deputation returned to the meeting, and reported the decision of the Tory Governor, the excitement became greater than ever. Suddenly, while the discussion was going on, a loud Indian war-whoop was heard in front of the church; this was replied to by another similar war-whoop from the gallery inside. It was evident that some mischief was on foot, that was not generally understood. This new development increased the agitation and alarm of the meeting. As it was now about six o'clock in the afternoon. The meeting adjourned. As the people passed out of the church, they saw to their surprise a number of Indians collected together. These directed their steps towards the wharf, followed by a large multitude. Presently the air began to resound with loud cries of 'Boston harbor a teapot! Boston harbor a teapot to-night!' This gave an inkling of what was going to be done, but those who were not in the secret hardly knew yet whether they ought to hinder the strange proceedings or help them on. The crowd pushed on in irregular procession until they reached Griffin's wharf. Here the 'Indians' went on board the vessels, followed by about a hundred and twenty others, some of whom had blackened their faces so as not to be recognised. Others, more bold or reckless, make no effort at concealment. And now the work of destruction began."

"And you were one of those Indians yourself, Uncle Tim?" repeated Tommy Brown, wonderingly.

"I was one of the Indians myself, little boy."

"What made you think of such a funny make-believe — and where did you all start from in the first place?"

"Why, about twenty of us had agreed beforehand to disguise ourselves, so as not to be detected by the officers of the government; and we decided it would be best to look like Mohawks. We were to take the lead in destroying the tea. I went in my disguise to the meeting in the Old South church, and stationed myself in the front gallery, near one of the windows, so that I could see what was passing in the streets; and when I saw the others make their appearance disguised as I was, I knew, you see, that the time for action had come. The war-whoop was the understood signal between us. When I answered it from the gallery, they knew word had come to the meeting from the Governor, that he would not let the vessels sail without landing their tea in America. That refusal, of course, put an end to all hopes of settling the difficulty in a friendly way. Well, as I was saying, when the Indians and their followers got aboard the ships, the work of destruction commenced. In all, there were about a hundred and forty of us, and there were no idle hands that night, either."

"What did you do first?" asked Bobby.

"Why, we first opened the hatches; then some went down into the holds of the vessels, and fastened the boxes of tea to the ropes; others on the deck hoisted them up, and as soon as they got possession of them they knocked a hole in them, and spilled the tea overboard into the water."

"I should suppose they would have wanted to carry home some of it to their grandmothers," suggested Tommy.

"Ah, yes; several sly fellows in the company *did* fill their pockets and *their shoes* as full as they could; and then there were a good many men in small boats who picked up some of the half-emptied boxes before they became entirely soaked with salt-water. But, boys, they had to use that tea very secretly, for any one detected with the article would have been mistrusted of having a hand in the riot. Besides, no good patriot would leave an American in peace with English tea in his possession after that — if he found it out. Those who got any of it that night had to hide it, therefore, in all sorts of out-of-the-way places."

"Didn't any of you get found out?"

"Not till it was too late to be any danger to

us; though I came pretty near it, for after the affair was over I returned home, and went to bed without looking sharp to see what I had brought with me. In the morning, as soon as my wife saw my stockings, she exclaimed, 'Why, Timothy, where did you go last night, to get your stockings *so full of tobacco?*'

"I tell you, boys, I shook those stockings out of the window in smart time — and I didn't stop shaking and brushing till I had cleaned the woolen of every tell-tale leaf. The good lady, you see, thought the tea was cut-tobacco! I was careless in not examining those long stockings before I went into the house. I might have known that some of the contraband stuff would stick to them. My cap, feathers, and other Indian gear, I managed to take off in the darkness as soon as I left the vessel, and threw them into the water."

"Didn't your wife ask any more questions about your stockings after that?" asked Bobby.

"Oh, she was puzzled, rather. But somehow

I hushed her up, and if she had any suspicions she was safe, and she kept me so by saying nothing. Well, that was the way, boys, that we made Boston Harbor a teapot, and defied the tyranny that forced taxes on us. And now, whenever you look on that picture you have in your hand, you'll set twice as much by it as you did before, for you know one of the 'Indians,' and he has explained it to you himself."

"That's true," said both the boys.

"How much tea was there, Uncle Tim?" persevered Tommy Brown, reluctant to leave the subject.

"Three hundred and forty-two chests, and we were only about three hours at it. You may believe we worked hard, but we did it with a good will, for we were working for our liberty."

The boys would gladly have tarried longer, and asked more questions, but some of their companions called for them, and they bade the old soldier good-bye till "the next time."

CHAPTER V.

LEXINGTON AND CONCORD.

A FEW days after Uncle Tim's narrative of the Boston Tea-Party, the same group of children were clustered around him again. The conversation at this time happened to turn upon the battles of Lexington and Concord.

"You see, boys," said the old soldier, "when the British Parliament saw that the Yankees had a will of their own, and wouldn't obey their unjust and tyrannical laws, they sent over more red-coats, a whole army of them, with plenty of muskets, cannon, and powder and shot, thinking to subdue us completely. They called us 'rebels,' and they calculated that their famous army was going to scare our 'rebellion' out of us, right away.

"Ah, boys, King George and his wise folks over there had studied the wrong dictionary that time. What they called 'rebellion' was the spirit of liberty, and they might as well have tried to drive salt out of the sea as to drive the spirit of liberty out of the Yankees. But they didn't know that as well then as they did a little while afterwards," continued the old man, with a pleasant smile and a slight chuckle. "When they had tried our metal seven years they were glad enough to cry quits, and let us alone. Yankee grit gave them something to chew on that they couldn't learn to like."

"What do you mean by that?" asked Bobby.

"Why, I mean that when they kept on trying to make us go down on our knees to 'em, and got only powder and ball for their pains, every time, it was worse to 'em than chewing gravel."

"I guess it was," responded the little boy.

"I'd ruther have my mouth filled chock full of sand, any time, than have bullets shot into my body."

"Well, Yankee grit run mostly in the shape of bullets, as the king's soldiers found it," said Uncle Tim. "And now for the story of the battle of Lexington.

"The Americans had collected some guns and ammunition, and stored them up in Concord, a small town about sixteen miles from Boston. General Gage, who had command of the British army that was stationed in Boston, heard of this, and he determined to capture or destroy these stores, so that our folks couldn't use 'em against the British. Early in the morning of the nineteenth of April, 1775, the general sent off Colonel Smith and Major Pitcairn, with about eight hundred men, the bravest and most experienced of the English army, to frighten the rebels, and make them give up the forbidden property. They expected to get away secretly in the dark, and be well on their way to Concord before the

Yankees were up. But they were mistaken. They didn't know us half so well in them days as we knew them. Our young General Warren was a man that got up too early for the British pretty generally, and that morning in particular he was up and dressed, and wide awake. And so when that British regiment was making its way along through Cambridge, and off into the country towards Concord, he knew all about it, and had guessed what they were up to, in fact, a good while before they started."

"Were you a soger then?" inquired little Tom.

"Why, yes, a sort of one, as I may say. You see, boys, all of us were soldiers then. We had no real, regular army, but every man that had a gun or a pistol, or a *pitchfork*, for that matter, got it out, and stood ready to meet the enemies of his country. I belonged to the Cambridge minute-men, and we had plenty to do that day, I'll warrant you. Well, as I was saying, the red-coats expected to get a good ways towards

Concord before the Americans could know it, and collect anywhere to dispute their passage. But 'the early bird' was too much for them. General Warren sent two men right into the country along the two different roads to Concord, to alarm the inhabitants, and have them prepared for what might follow. One of these messengers, William Davis, crossed Boston neck, and went through Brookline to Lexington; the other, Paul Revere, went through Charlestown and Cambridge. Revere came near being caught. He met in Charlestown two British officers on horseback. They hailed him and wanted him to stop, but he had other business, and so he just wheeled his horse around and darted off at his highest speed. The officers commenced following him. One of them being adroitly deceived by Revere, plunged into a slough, and got nothing for his pains but muddy clothes."

"And what became of the other?" asked several boys, laughing.

"Why, you see, Revere knew the different

roads, and so, slipping into the one that led to Medford, he got out of the way before the officer knew where he was going.

"As he passed on he alarmed every house, and waked up all the families. 'The British are coming! the British are coming!' he shouted, as his horse's feet clattered along the road. Children cried, women turned pale (though most of them were terribly resolute), and the men seized their guns and powder-horns, and prepared for the worst. The consequence was, that, when the red-coats got into the country, they found the Yankees were all aware of their coming, and were prepared to receive them. Guns were firing, bells were ringing, and everybody, young and old, was astir. Colonel Smith saw how it was, and sent back to Boston for more troops. There was need of it. Ministers, and gray-haired grandfathers, and even half-grown boys, were mustering on all sides for the coming conflict. As I said, we had no real army organized, then, and we didn't march by trained companies.

But you may guess we minute-men were off for Concord early that morning.

"I seized my old gun as soon as the alarm came, and, slinging my cartridge-box and powder-horn, too, I took the war-path, not knowing whether I'd ever come back. Ha! I remember what my wife said to me at the door."

"What was it, Uncle Tim?"

"Bless you! the women were the very soul of courage, and as full o' liberty as the men — if not more. Says my wife, 'Timothy, don't you flinch! If you want more cartridges I'll make them for you. If you get out of bullets I'll melt the pewter spoons.' I tell you, boys, with that ringing in my ears, I couldn't be a sheep when the fight came.

"Well, on the way to Lexington, we fell in with plenty more bound on the same errand — and we didn't let grass grow under our feet. But before we got to the town, *their* minute-men had got the news, and were paraded on the common, under Capt. John Parker. Captain Parker ordered the company to load their guns with powder and ball, but not to fire till the British gave the first shot. After setting sentinels, he dismissed the company with orders to meet again at the call of the drum. Some went to their homes, and some lingered around the tavern."

"Was it daylight, then?" asked Tommy.

"No," said Uncle Tim, "there was scarcely a streak of gray in the sky yet.

"After the company had scattered, and some had made up their minds that it was all a false alarm, one of the sentinels, watching down the road, discovered a British officer coming, and instantly fired his gun. Soon alarm-guns were heard in all directions. The church-bell tolled, and the drum-roll called back the minute-men at double-quick. Then for the first time we began to smell battle. There was work in earnest now just ahead. Liberty or death! Some of us surmised that, as Samuel Adams and John Hancock, who were known by the British to be strong sons of liberty, lived in Lexington, perhaps the design of the British in coming there was to seize these men! If they succeeded in this they would be sure to hang them. So we persuaded the two patriots to retire to Woburn, a few miles off. We had hard work to make them go, for they burned to meet the brunt of the battle with us. But we told them their lives were worth more to us than a host of common men, and they must not run any risks. After they had gone, we heard the Red-coats coming. How insulting they were! They marched up, playing *Yankee Doodle!* The rascals knew that nothing could mock us more than for them to take our pet tune and fife it in our faces in ridicule. They soon stopped their music, however. Hearing the alarms, and getting sight of the minute-men, they probably concluded they would meet with some opposition. So they halted to get their arms ready, and to wait for the main body to come up. In the meantime, about sixty or seventy of the minute-men had been drawn up on the common in two ranks. Brave hearts we all had, but the suspense was trying enough, waiting there for the regulars to attack us. A little before sunrise they all made their appearance. First came the advance guard, and behind them the tall grenadiers with their high caps. They marched almost on a run — eight hundred or more drilled and picked soldiers against seventy farmers with no military training or experience whatever! But *they didn't scare us!* There we stood and waited for them, rushing right at us with their scarlet coats and feathers, and gleaming guns. Major Pitcairn rode in front, and when he got to within about five rods of us, he yelled out, 'Disperse, disperse, you rebels! lay down your arms, and disperse!'"

"Did you go?" asked Bobby, with his eyes stretched uncommonly wide.

"No, we stood still, just as if we didn't hear what he said."

"What did the major do then?"

"He was mad as a sore dog. He whipped

out his pistol, and hallooed louder, 'Why don't you lay down your arms and disperse?' but we were determined not to go till we were forced to, so we didn't answer, and we didn't run. When the major saw that we didn't move, he discharged his pistol and ordered his men to fire. Immediately a deadly volley poured in upon us at close range. If they had aimed like marksmen they'd have killed every man!"

"Did you run, then?" asked half a dozen breathless listeners.

"It was suicide to stay there and be shot down — a handful of sixty or seventy against an army! The British had fired the first shot, and we fired back and retreated. Our captain, Jonas Parker, was as brave a man as ever carried a gun. He said before the battle he never would run from the Britishers, and he stuck to his word. After firing his gun, a wound from the enemy brought him almost to the ground. But he rallied enough to commence reloading his piece, when one of the bloody red-coats rushed upon him, and stabbed him dead upon the spot with his bayonet!"

"Did anybody else get killed?" asked Tommy, pitifully.

"Yes. Jonathan Harrington was mortally wounded right in front of the house where he lived. And what made it more dreadful, his wife was looking at him from the window when he fell. Poor man! he managed to crawl as far as the door, whilst the blood was streaming from his breast, and there he breathed his last! He had just been in the meeting-house after some powder, when the shot hit him."

"How many were killed in all, Uncle Tim?"

"There were seven killed and nine wounded. There was weeping and wailing that day in Lexington."

"But didn't you kill any of the Britishers?"

"Not on the spot. But we paid them well before night. I thought to myself when I saw the men fall, 'As sure as God is just, these red-coats will get their reward.'"

"How did they?"

"After they had succeeded in scattering this handful of patriots on Lexington common, they marched for Concord. But the minute-men were prepared to receive them there, too. They had a skirmish there. But the British succeeded in destroying some public stores. They spiked two cannon; burnt the liberty-pole, and several artillery carriages; threw five hundred pounds of ball into the mill-pond, and broke up sixty barrels of flour. But as good luck would have it, they broke these barrels in such a bungling way that the people succeeded in saving one-half the flour. The other stores had been concealed, so that the enemy could not find them, though I tell you, boys, they hadn't much time to search. Affairs were getting hotter for them every minute, and they soon commenced their retreat."

"What! did they get beaten?" asked Bob.

"Well, boys," replied Uncle Tim, "I guess

that before night-fall they felt about as well-beaten as any retreating army ever was."

"Good!" exclaimed the boys. "They'd no business to shoot the Americans down and steal and destroy their things."

"But how did you beat them at last?" quoth practical little Bob.

"Why, it was known all along the road that they had killed some Americans, and that excited the people terribly; and then we were receiving additions to our number every hour from all the surrounding towns. When these recruits came in and saw the killed and wounded, and the women and children crying around them, it stirred up all their righteous vengeance, and they vowed they would retaliate on some of the murderers. So when the red-coats began to retreat towards Boston, the patriots ran through the fields and ambushed them along the roads, and picked them off with musket shots, man after man, so that really that day ended with one of the most disastrous flights of the British during the whole war.

"While these sharp-shooters, singly and in squads, were wounding and killing them from behind walls, rocks and thickets on the way, some of our men hung upon the rear of the enemy, and shot them as often as they got within range. Of course the British were firing at us during all their flight, and we had to be very cautious. It was a kind of running battle all the way from Concord to Cambridge. As they retreated, the British not only fired at our men, but rushed into the houses; killed some who were there, and in a number of instances they set the houses on fire. But we followed so close behind that we could generally put out the fires. Major Pitcairn himself narrowly escaped being taken prisoner that day. He was obliged to leave his horse. We captured that, and found that Pitcairn had left in such haste that he hadn't time to take the pistols out of their holsters. He must have been brought to very close quarters, just then. Well, when the red-coats had gone as far as Cambridge, there they were met by Lord Percy, who had come out with another detachment from Boston to help them. Percy formed his soldiers into a large, hollow square, and into this hollow square we drove the retreating red-coats like a flock of sheep into a fold. It was lucky for them that Percy came as he did, for, what with fighting and running, they were almost ready to fall down in the road from sheer fatigue. As soon as the fugitive troops found themselves protected, they threw themselves on the ground with their tongues hanging out of their mouths, and panted like so many hunted-down deer. Concord-day was a dreadful one for *that* regiment of red-coats."

"Do you know how many were killed and wounded, Uncle Tim?"

"On our side there were forty-nine killed, and thirty-four wounded," replied the old man.

"Was that more than the red-coats lost?"

"No, no, my boys; nor half so many, either. Their killed, wounded and missing numbered *two hundred and seventy-three!* We called it a victory, for we drove the British into Boston, and kept them there. Well, the news of that day's bloody work went throughout the colonies like wild-fire, and nerved the whole country at once to the work of common defence. The war was begun. Volunteers came pouring in from all parts, so that *for numbers* we soon had quite a respectable army. We were badly equipped and poorly supplied for an eight years' war. But, boys, the Great Jehovah was with us, and he gave us the victory."

"Hulloo! there's a red-coat!" cried little Bobby, as he pointed to a sailor in the street who had a dancing monkey dressed in a red flannel jacket. "Let's go and see him!" and away scampered the children to see this new curiosity, leaving the old soldier alone.

CHAPTER VI.

THE GREEN MOUNTAIN BOYS.

On the night of the 9th of May, 1775, a keen observer might have descried half a dozen or more boats rowing stealthily through the darkness across Lake Champlain on their way to Fort Ticonderoga. The boats were filled with some eighty-three Green Mountain Boys, who, under the command of Ethan Allen, had set out to capture that strong fortress, and take possession of the cannon and military stores which were known to be there. The object of this party was not to fight, but to get possession of the fort and its garrison by stratagem. There was no time, therefore, to send for the rear-guard on the other side of the lake.

It was decided to make the attack at once. One of the leading officers of this small force was Benedict Arnold. He had received a commission as colonel from the Committee of Safety, in Boston, to raise and take command of a company of four hundred men. It was therefore natural, perhaps, that he should feel himself entitled to head this important expedition, and, prompted besides by his personal ambition, he at first insisted upon it. But to this the Green Mountain boys would not consent. They were determined that their leader should be their friend and neighbor, Ethan Allen, under whom they had first enlisted; and they would go with no one else. Finally it was arranged that Arnold and Allen should advance to the attack side by side. On the shore of the lake, after midnight, the men were drawn up in three ranks. As the undertaking was one of great uncertainty, and might prove also one of great peril, Allen wanted none but brave hearts to accompany him. He therefore determined to give any who felt in the least reluctant or timid, an opportunity to remain behind. He addressed them as follows:

"Friends and fellow-soldiers: we must this morning quit our pretensions to valor, or possess ourselves of this fort. But it will be a dangerous and desperate undertaking, and I do not urge any one to join in it *against his will*. You that will go with us *voluntarily*, poise your firelocks!"

His call for volunteers was answered unanimously. Every man poised his firelock, and Allen's eyes sparkled with delight when he saw the spirit of his company.

"Face to the right," he cried, and taking the lead of the centre file, with Arnold by his side, he marched towards the fort. When he reached the large gate he found it shut, but a small wicket was fortunately open. But here was a wide-awake sentry, who, when he saw the

Yankees approaching, levelled his piece at Allen, and snapped it. But the gun would not go off. Finding himself disarmed, the sentry then retreated through a covered way to the "parade-ground," within the fortress inclosure. The Green-Mountain Boys followed him, and he proved a good guide. Once in the fort, the Americans rushed upon the guards, shouting, yelling, and sounding their Indian whoop, and then they formed on the parade-ground in such a manner as to face and guard each of the barracks, where the garrison lay. One of the sentinels wounded an American officer, but being wounded in return, he cried, "Quarter! quarter!"

"If I spare you, will you show me the apartment of your commander?" said Ethan Allen.

"I will."

"Lead on, then."

The sentinel went forward, and Allen followed. When he reached the commander's door, Allen cried out to him:

"Come forth instantly, or I will sacrifice the whole garrison."

At this summons the commander, whose name was Delaplace, made his appearance in a very unsoldierly plight. Having been aroused in such haste, he had no time to dress, and so presented himself before Allen with his breeches in his hand.

"Deliver to me this fort instantly," said Allen.

"By what authority?" asked the astonished officer.

"In the name of the Great Jehovah and of the Continental Congress!" cried the impatient Vermonter.

Delaplace was about to remonstrate, or possibly make further inquiries, but Allen peremptorily stopped him, and shook his sword over the commander's head. Delaplace, seeing it was useless to parley or resist, at once surrendered the fort, and ordered all the soldiers under his command to parade without arms. By the time the sun was fairly up, that important stronghold, which had cost the British millions of dollars, and many brave lives, was in the possession of the Americans. A mere handful of undisciplined Green Mountain Boys had taken it in ten minutes without the loss of a man. It was a bold and skilful exploit, and greatly exalted Allen in the estimation of his countrymen.

The importance of this victory may be inferred from the fact that it put in possession of the Americans fifty prisoners, more than a hundred pieces of cannon, a number of swivels, and a large quantity of small arms and ammunition —of which last the colonists were then very much in need.

CHAPTER VII.

BUNKER HILL.

There had been a military display in the streets of New York. It was the anniversary of the seventeenth of June. Our young lads had been down to the Battery to see the parade, and on their way home, as they passed Uncle Tim's house, they saw him sitting in his great cane-bottomed chair, in his usual place in the door-yard.

"Well, boys," said the old man, "the soldiers made a fine show to-day. It did my old eyes good to look at them. I hope the time'll never come when Americans will forgot to celebrate this day."

"I think Fourth o' July's better, Uncle Tim," said a shrill, boyish voice.

"Maybe you're right, Benny, but Seventeenth o' June prepared the way for Fourth o' July. The two days are kind o' sisters, you see. The Revolution was the mother of 'em both, and I believe they're the two brightest births marked in her almanac.

"Do you see that new cloth sign on the hotel over there?" asked the old soldier, pointing to a transparency which had been put up in front of the public house opposite.

"Yes, sir," replied the lads, in chorus.

"Well, what does it say?"

"Bunker Hill."

"Short enough; but it tells a long story — at least to men like me, who helped do the fighting there. That name can't mean the same to you that it does to an old soldier; but I want you always to shout for it when the seventeenth of June comes round. Now, boys, I can give you something to remember about it. Want to hear about the great battle, and the burning o' Charlestown, and about General Warren, and old Put?"

"Yes, yes!" shouted all the eager group.

"Well, then, come round here and keep still. You see there was no help for it, and we must come to a downright set-to with them English red-coats sooner or later. Everything they did in the name o' the king provoked us, and everything we did in the name o' liberty made them mad. They had possession of Boston, and we had possession of all outside of Boston. They wanted to push into the country to plunder and kill, and we knew it, and kept watch. The patriots laid siege to Boston, and hemmed 'em in there for weeks. But about the middle of June, after they had received a large addition of soldiers from England, with a number of brave generals, we saw from the movements of their troops that they were preparing to attack us. So our leaders held a council of war in Cambridge, and talked over several plans, and

General Putnam advised them to occupy Bunker Hill, and plant cannon there to hold the British in check, and more easily keep them where they were. The result was that an order came from headquarters to Colonel Prescott, to take a thousand Yankee soldiers and fortify Bunker Hill. All that is as fresh to me as yesterday, — and how grimly and quietly the companies mustered, and how solemnly good Mr. Langdon prayed with us on Cambridge common before we started. 'Twas a warm, starlight night when we commenced the march over to the Neck. We didn't want the enemy to know what we were doing, and so we chose to go in the dark."

"Were you a reg'lar army, then?" asked Benny.

"No. The British were well supplied with the best of everything used in war. They were splendidly drilled; they had their commissioned officers, beautiful uniforms, and plenty of powder and ball. But our soldiers were the farmers and mechanics who had but lately come from their work, some with rifles, some with " Queen Ann " muskets, and old powder-horns; some with nothing but hatchets, pitchforks or clubs. We had on uniforms, no feathers, — nothing that made us *look* like soldiers. Besides, we had no regular officers, and but little ammunition. And yet, boys, every man that marched to Bunker Hill that night WAS a soldier, though he carried a stick and went in his shirt-sleeves, — as many of us did. Never went braver hearts to battle than beat in the bosoms of those minute-men. We all felt the strength of *a good cause*, and the blessing of a just God; and, defending our rights for the sake of our families and our country, there couldn't be a coward amongst us."

"Did you *fight* in the dark?" asked little Bobby, impatient of a slight pause, during which the old warrior communed with his thoughts.

"No, my little lad. The enemy did not discover us, and we had as much as we could do to prepare for fighting, — though we common soldiers didn't know that till we reached the spot. Arrived at Bunker Hill, we saw the wagons and the spades, and then the leaders told us what we had to do. But now the question rose, whether Bunker Hill was really the best place to begin. Putnam and Prescott discussed the matter, and saw that there would be a difficulty. Cannons planted here would not be of much use unless we went down to the end of the peninsula nearer Boston, where the enemy were, and fortified that, too. Bunker Hill was *too far off*. The orders were to entrench there, but in those raw-militia days circumstances altered orders sometimes. 'Push on to *Breed's* Hill,' says Putnam to Prescott; 'we'll fortify that *first*.' This was bold counsel, and boldly followed; Breed's Hill was an advance post, and almost under the very noses of the British."

"Was it far from Bunker Hill?" asked Benny.

"No, only a little way. It is in the eastern part of Charlestown, directly opposite the city of Boston, across the channel where the sea comes in. So on to Breed's Hill we went. As soon as we reached the top (about midnight), we began to dig our entrenchments, and throw up a 'redoubt' (a sort of pen fenced with banks of earth), to protect us from the guns of the British. This was done with just as little noise as possible, so that the enemy should not hear us. Oh, how we worked! We knew we must get the whole done before morning, or lose our labor; for as soon as daylight showed the British where we were, they would let loose all their artillery on us.

"Col. Gridley planned the entrenchments, and took hold and dug with the rest of us; and I saw Col. Prescott and Gen. Putnam at work, too. We all laid to it with such good will, and made such dispatch, that we had our breastworks up and guns planted by day-break. Not a minute too early, I assure you. As soon as it was light enough, the English sentries saw us, and then the war-dogs began to bark, the alarm-guns roused the whole British army, — and all the citizens of Boston and Charlestown, too. Most of the people got up a good deal earlier that morning than usual."

"Were the war-dogs *real* dogs that the British had?" inquired wondering little Bobby.

"No," said Uncle Tim, with a hearty laugh, in which all the older boys joined, "I meant the cannon. We call them 'war-dogs,' sometimes. The cannon that first sent their compliments over to us were on board the ships of war that lay in the water around Boston and Charlestown. Later, they began to fire at us from Copp's Hill Fort in Boston. But we worked on, for there was more to be done before we would be in any condition to meet the red-coats when they came over to attack us in force.

"It was a terribly hot day, and the sweltering sun, and the enemy's balls hailing round us, made our situation distressing enough. We had to swallow our rations between shots, and get our water as we could, or go without. Early in the forenoon, one poor fellow, digging by my side, was hit by a ball and fell dead in his tracks. Some of the new recruits began to be nervous, but Colonel Prescott, to inspire them with courage, mounted the embankment, where he could be easily seen by the British, and walked slowly backwards and forwards, bareheaded, giving us orders, and overseeing our work as coolly as if he'd been inspecting us at dress-parade. I heard afterwards that General Gage saw him plainly, with a telescope, from Boston. Willard, who was Prescott's brother-in-law, was standing by General Gage at the time.

"'Who *is* that bald-headed man walking to and fro on the parapet?' asked Gage.

"Willard looked through the telescope, and said:

"'It is Colonel William Prescott.'

"'Will he fight?' inquired Gage.

"'Yes,' said Willard, 'to the last drop of his blood.'

"The old colonel's brave bearing made us all

braver. With such examples in our leaders, and with our own stout hearts, *fear* was the least of our troubles. Our worst torment was want of water."

"Why couldn't you get water?" asked Tommy Brown."

"After the firing commenced, the only well we stood any chance of using was back on the Neck, and it was a costly job to get a drink there, let alone carrying a bucket-full. The cannons on the ships swept the whole peninsula. I never was so dry in my life. It seemed as if I should die of thirst sometimes — and that was the way most of us felt.

"After having sweat and worked so hard all night, and eaten so little, I tell you we weren't in the best o' condition to fight them lusty redcoats, with their full stomachs, and their good night's rest. But we were determined to fight, all the same.

"When the entrenchments on Breed's Hill were finished, Old Put, who had been riding back and forth ever since daybreak, to get supplies from headquarters, and hurry up reinforcements, headed a detachment of our men to Bunker Hill, to throw up some earthworks there. They took our tools with them, and began to dig; and the general worked like a beaver to keep 'em at it with good courage. But they were too tired and spent, and the British fire galled them terribly. A little after noon, Putnam was wanted elsewhere, and had to go; and then the poor fellows scattered, and most of 'em never came back to help us again. About one o'clock we saw the British soldiers coming across the channel in a great many small boats; they landed, and as soon as all of them were ready, they commenced to march up the hill straight towards us, the artillery firing from the ships and the Boston forts all the time.

"We lay behind our breastworks, watching the red platoons come on. They marched with steady step, with banners flying, and their polished weapons flashing in the sun. It was a formidable sight.

"In the meantime, Prescott and Putnam came around, and cheered up the men.

"'Boys,' says the colonel, 'the red-coats will never reach this redoubt if you'll obey orders. Keep your fire till I give the word, and be careful *not to shoot over their heads!*'

"'Save your powder, boys,' says Putnam, 'it's scarce, and mustn't be wasted. Aim low, and *as soon as we can see the whites of their eyes,* you'll hear the order to fire!'

"And Stark and brave old Pomeroy repeated these directions in other parts of the line. As the British came nearer they opened on us with heavy volleys of musketry, but these did no harm. They only rung the first bell for the death-meeting. And now the shores of Boston, and all the house-tops and windows through the north and west end of the town were filled with people, looking at the sight. The moment of battle had come."

"I should s'pose,' said Tommy, "you would a' been so fierce to shoot that you couldn't a' held in, anyhow."

"I tell you we *were* fierce for it," replied Uncle Tim, with animation; "we fairly ached to begin the firing, the enemy were getting so near, and showed such a splendid mark; and we there waiting with loaded guns, all primed and cocked and aimed. But all of us that were in the redoubt managed to keep quiet. A few marksmen in the earthworks on our left did let off their shot, but Old Put rode up to them in a fury, and threatened to cut them down with his sword if they didn't obey orders.

"The British had got within seven or eight rods when the word was given to fire; and right on the echo every musket and rifle spoke. All along our own entrenchments was one line of red blaze and blue smoke, and a stream of hot bullets poured into the enemy, mowing them down like grass. The English army never had met such a volley before. There was scarcely a man in their van that wasn't killed or wounded. Oh, it was a sight to see! whole heaps of men lying there on the turf, officers and soldiers together, groaning and writhing, or deadly still! The shock was such to all the red-coat troops that their leaders couldn't do anything with them. They showed their backs to us, and ran down the hill."

"You beat 'em, didn't you?" cried the young listeners.

"We did *that* time, most decidedly."

"Was that the end of the battle?"

"No, no! the British officers were unwilling to give it up, and let the Yankees have the day. So they rallied their men; but it took them some time to get ready to come up that hill again."

"Just now the battle took on a new horror. We had begun to see smoke rolling up to the right of us from some of the houses in Charlestown, but we hadn't realized till now that the whole place was burning. General Howe had given the cruel order, and gunners on Copp's

Hill had flung bomb-shells over into the town, and some marines from the Somerset helped on the rascally work, till the fire was set in so many places that it swept all afore it. Some of our men had homes and families in Charlestown, and you must guess how they felt. We all grew furious at the outrage, and gritted our teeth, and vowed to make the British pay for it before night.

"It was an awful spectacle — that flaming town close by, let alone our grief and gloom at the loss. We had too much hot work in hand to spend time looking at it, but when the church-spire caught and blazed into the sky, one glance was enough to make us remember it forever. There it stood, America's first liberty-pole — a pillar of fire!

"Well, after a while the British got ready, and marched up the hill again. We waited this time till they were within *six* rods of us, and then we gave them another volley as terrible as the first. When the wind blew the smoke away there they lay all along the ground, like swathes of red clover. But the royalist officers were getting desperate now. It would mortify them terribly to retreat again. They pushed on their other platoons, and kept them firing their guns at us, and at the same time the cannon from the ships and the fort were pouring their balls into our works. But we stood our ground, and gave the red-coats such a hot reception that they could not get any nearer, try what they would. The officers cursed and yelled at their men, and struck them with the flat of their swords, but it was all in vain. In a few minutes they all broke in confusion, and fled like a scared mob, pell-mell down to the water, leaving their dead and wounded on the field. Scores of them were so panic-struck that they even scrambled into their boats, and were going to row back to Boston. When we saw the enemy scatter, we sent up such a shout of triumph as might have been heard for miles. It was a glorious moment! It almost paid us for the burning of Charlestown."

And the excited old hero paused to take breath, and wipe the sweat from his forehead.

"The battle was over, now, weren't it?" asked Benny.

"No, no, sonny. I wish it had been. Why, there were near five thousand British engaged against us that day. So there were enough left after all we had killed, and besides, our powder was beginning to give out now. Howe, and Clinton, and Pigot, and the rest of the officers got their scattered troops together once more. They had learned something this time, and had thrown away their heavy knapsacks, and came on without stopping to fire their muskets. Their field-pieces they managed to place so as to rake the *inside*, of our works, and then they attacked us on three sides at once. They marched with fixed bayonets, intending to charge. When they were within twenty yards of us, we poured upon them another dreadful shower of balls, cutting down a great many of them; but though they wavered for a few moments, they recovered and rushed upon us. It was a hand-to-hand fight now. All our ammunition was gone, and, as we had no bayonets, we used the butts of our guns to beat them back; but we couldn't — only fifteen hundred of us against so many. So we were forced to give way. General Warren was the last to leave the trenches, but he remained a little too long. Before he got off the hill he was slain. Prescott came near being killed, too. He remained until the red-coats could reach him with their bayonets. They made several attempts to stab him, but he parried their guns with his sword, and escaped, though not till his coat and waistcoat were torn into shreds."

"How many were killed, Uncle Tim?"

"On the part of the enemy there were over ten hundred and fifty killed and wounded. Seventy of these were officers. On our side we lost four hundred and forty-nine, killed, wounded and missing. Ah, my boys, if we'd only had a few reinforcements that day, or if our powder hadn't given out! As it was, though we lost the field, who says we didn't *win the day?*

"It was a battle that gained us glory and showed our strength; and the report of us that went through the country was the means of bringing out a great number to join our army. At the same time it convinced the English that we were a foe quite worthy of them, and not to be despised any more. After that they grew more cautious of giving us battle on our own ground. 'Bunker-hill Day' taught the British that the *Yankees could fight!*"

CHAPTER VIII.

THE SIEGE OF BOSTON.

On the evening of that same holiday, after supper, Tommy Brown, and his friends Ben and Bobby, finding no sport or game to occupy the long twilight quite to their mind, made their way again to the house of the old soldier, and begged him to tell them "some more war-stories."

"I don't know, I don't know," said the old man, "I'm afraid there ain't any story fit to tell on Bunker Hill day, but the story of Bunker Hill, and you've had that."

"Oh, Uncle Tim, you can tell us what the British did," said Ben.

"Well, I will. After that battle the British were afraid to push into the country lest they should be treated worse than they were when they went to Concord. They had found out how Yankee guns could kill, and didn't mean to risk any more till they were obliged to. They were ashamed to leave by water, for that would look as if they were beaten. So they staid in Boston. But it wasn't comfortable for them there, now. Washington had been appointed commander of the American army by Congress, and he wasn't the man to let a tyrant's troops stay peaceably in the cradle of liberty. He set a close seige round the town, and penned them in, and kept them in a state of alarm all the time. Meanwhile he organized his army and had them thoroughly drilled. This situation of affairs lasted several months."

"Why didn't Washington drive them out?" asked Tommy.

"He didn't for three or four reasons. In the first place, the other officers of the army advised him not to. Then there were our patriot families. To bombard the enemy, and dislodge them by fire and sword, would leave many loyal Boston people homeless. Finally, he was loth to destroy American property. Most of the buildings in Boston, and immense quantities of goods, belonged to our friends, and if Washington had attacked the town, a great deal of that property would have been destroyed. Besides, it wasn't known whether the Continental Congress would approve of it. But finally Washington got tired of simply watching the British. So he wrote to Congress and asked their opinion about bombarding Boston. When this letter was read to them, there was a solemn silence in the House. No one wanted to take the responsibility of recommending a measure that must cost Americans so much. John Hancock, one of the noblest patriots who ever lived, was then President of Congress. As he belonged to Boston, and owned much real estate there, one of the members of Congress proposed that he should

The house of John Hancock, Beacon Street, Boston.   Page 86.

give his opinion upon the subject first, being more personally interested than any one else. Mr. Hancock rose and said these words. I have always remembered them, boys, because they made such an impression on me the first time I read them. They speak the sentiment of a real patriot."

"'It is true,' said he, 'that I am personally interested in this question. Nearly all the property I have in the world, is in houses and other estate in the town of Boston; but if the expulsion of the British army from Boston, and the liberty of our country, require their being burnt to ashes, *issue the order for it immediately!*'"

"Well, by the middle of February, 1776, it was determined to attack the town, and drive the British out. So Washington ordered batteries to be planted on the surrounding heights, from which balls and bomb-shells could be thrown, and on the night of the second of March, they opened their fire. The storm of destruction came furious and fast, and the British soldiers had all they could do to put out the flames kindled by the siege artillery. The bombardment was continued all that night, and all the next day. On the night of March 4th, my regiment was ordered up to the top of Dorchester Heights, a couple o' miles south-east of Boston. I was under General Thomas then. The night was terribly dark, and the cold, bleak wind cut our faces cruelly. We marched without fife or drum, or any noise. When we had climbed the Heights we went at once to work digging entrenchments and erecting forts."

"Didn't that make you think of Bunker Hill?" said Ben.

"Yes; only the ground was froze, and it was ten times harder work. But it was cold enough to work hard, and we plied our picks and spades with right good will. War wasn't a mere *experiment* with us now. We had got drilled to it, and felt confident. Our army was larger and better equipped, and better supplied with guns and powder. Besides, we knew the British were about worried out. The siege had harassed them badly, and they weren't in near so good spirits as they were when they attacked us at Charlestown. Well, before morning, we had two forts on Dorchester Heights and guns all in position. When the sun rose, and the British saw what we had done, they were amazed. *They* thought of Bunker Hill, I'll warrant you. A remark that General Howe made there was reported to us afterwards, and we thought it was a great compliment."

"What was it, Uncle Tim?" asked little Bobby.

"When he saw our works there, begun and finished since last sundown, says he, crossly enough, 'Them rebels have done more in one night, than my army would have done in a week!'"

"Did he try to drive you off?"

"Yes. He took two thousand of his troops — picked men all of them — got them into boats and commenced rowing towards us across the harbor."

"Did you have another battle?" asked Benny.

"No, Providence prevented it; for the wind blew so strong, and the waves rolled so high, that it was impossible for them to cross. So they had to return. The next day General Howe called a counsel of war. He got his officers together and asked them what they thought it was best to do. They told him the best thing he could do was to get out of Boston. This was agreed upon at last. But it took them several days to get ready. Whilst they were lingering, our folks one night erected another fort and battery on another hill in Dorchester, called Nook's Hill. From this fort they could not only send balls and bombs into Boston, but they could also rake Boston Neck. When the British saw this, it made 'em feel in a great hurry to get away. They saw there was no time to trifle. So the select men of Boston (Tories, of course) sent a flag of truce to Washington, and told him that General Howe with all his red-coats was going to leave the town, and if the Americans wouldn't fire on them the British would promise not to do any damage to the public property. Washington was too wise to pledge himself not to fire, but he made 'em some answer that satisfied 'em. It was the eighteenth of March, before the British got ready to go; but on that day, at four in the morning, General Howe, with his army of ten thousand men, went on board the English ships that were in the harbor and set sail for Halifax. Just as the last company left the dock, the Americans marched into the city with their flags flying and their bands playing Yankee Doodle. That was a happy day to us, boys, and also to the patriot people. How they cheered, and how the girls and women waved their handkerchiefs as we marched through the streets! They hailed us as their deliverers, and many in our ranks were their fathers, and husbands, and brothers, too. There was singing, playing and bell-ringing, and great joy everywhere, in Boston that night."

"Were all the people who had lived in Boston, there, then?"

"No, my boy. A good many of the people took sides with the British, and when the red-coats left the city these Tories went with them to Halifax. They carried with them all the property they could, but they had to leave a good deal behind, and that they lost. The army, too, lost not a little, for they left behind them a large amount of military stores, which our soldiers were very glad to get."

"What were these stores, Uncle Tim?" asked practical Tommy.

"Why, as there were fifteen hundred tory families who went away with the Red-coats, the vessels were not large enough to take everything, so they had to leave two hundred and fifty pieces of cannon, four large mortars for throwing bombs, a hundred and fifty horses, twenty-five thousand bushels of wheat, and I don't know how much barley, oats, and other provisions which we greatly needed. And that isn't all, boys, either," and the old soldier paused, and looked exultant.

"Oh, tell us the rest," cried all his hearers together.

"You see, after the British army had left Boston, several store-ships from England, laden with quantities of articles that an army might need, arrived in the harbor; and the captains of the vessels didn't know that we'd driven the British away, so they sailed right up to the wharf, and we seized 'em, and took possession of everything they brought, and the officers and crew too."

"Did they have any powder on board?" inquired Ben.

"Yes, one of them had fifteen hundred barrels of powder, besides solid shot and plenty of guns and other war material."

"Were there any soldiers among 'em?"

"One of the vessels had seven hundred soldiers aboard right from Britian."

"What did you do with *them?*" quoth little Bob.

"We took 'em prisoners, and kept 'em till we could exchange 'em for Americans which the British had taken, or might take from us during the war."

CHAPTER IX.

THE UNEXPECTED GUEST.

It was during the beautiful month of June, in one of the early years of the Revolutionary war, that an old farmer and his wife sat one warm afternoon in front of their old-fashioned house on the banks of the Hudson River, alternately talking and dozing. From their little door-yard they could see the grand river for many miles, but above it was cut off by a sudden bend which carried it behind a high mountain. The splendor of the declining sun had gradually veiled itself, and was now beginning to darken in the shadow of distant thunder-clouds.

The old man roused himself, wondering if night could have come upon him so unawares.

"Look at Old Tom," said he (meaning the neighboring mountain). "Look at Old Tom, he's drawing a black night-cap on his head."

The old woman started from her incipient nap, and seeing the clouds, muttered something, and began to look for the knitting-work she had dropped.

Far different from the two prosy characters in the little door-yard scene, both in seeming and in fact, was the lonely rider a few miles below, who at that very time was cautiously approaching the river through the wild hills, looking keenly about him. He was a tall, nobly-formed man, mounted on a fine horse. A single glance at his military bearing and his peculiar manner would have convinced one that he was there reconnoitering the condition and movements of the British, for his position was not far from their lines. It was while he was engaged in this important but perilous duty that a company of the enemy who were scouring the country in search of cattle for food suddenly came in sight. The American had gone deeper into danger than he supposed. No sooner did the foraging party espy him than with shouts and savage oaths they dashed forward to take him prisoner or shoot him in his saddle.

The stranger put spurs to his horse and darted away, swift as a native deer. Out of the glen, up the hill, he rode, shaping his course toward a neighboring wood, amid whose trees he expected to conceal himself. His pursuers followed him hotly, yelling, cursing, and firing their carbines; but they could neither overtake nor hit him. In a few minutes the forest was reached. The stranger seemed well acquainted with the paths, and taking one of these, he pushed rapidly into the shadow. His enraged pursurers soon lost him among the trees and underwood, and were obliged to give up the chase. After riding some time at full speed the American reined up his horse, and hearing nothing of the enemy behind him proceeded at a leisurely walk.

The gathering darkness had deceived him in the forest, but now the muttering of distant thunder explained it. This was followed by loud rumblings, and presently a sharp flash of lightning admonished him to quicken his steps. Patting the horse's neck and speaking a few kind words to him, he put him again to his speed. Great drops of rain splashed down upon him as he fled, and then the water came in torrents, accompanied by furious gusts of wind that drove the pelting vollies direct into the traveler's face. He kept on, but it was a tedious progress, and before long the added darkness of real night set in. Our hero found it almost impossible to proceed, and guiding his horse under the thick foliage of an old oak, he was preparing to spend the night there, when his eye detected the faint glimmerin' of a light. He cautiously approached it, and found that it proceeded from a farm house. Prudently looking through the window he saw only an old man and woman, and felt sure that they were the only inmates. He could hear their voices in the pauses of the thunder, for though the storm had somewhat abated, it was wild weather still, outside.

"The cow-boys* won't be ransacking round to-night, eh, goody?" quoth the old man.

"Why, I don't know — I'll ventur' it's the very sort o' night they like best," replied his wife. "Hark! what's that?"

"Oh, that's only the window-sash ratt—"

Here three distinct knocks on the door interrupted the speaker, and suddenly changed his opinion. "Fact!" he muttered, half to himself. "There's somebody there. Wonder who 'tis."

"Whoever 'tis, I'm 'fraid we'll wish him furder," fluttered the old lady, standing up very straight, and looking nervous.

The farmer went to the door. "Who's there?" said he, shouting through the key-hole.

"A friend, who has lost his way, and needs a shelter."

* Gangs of tory outlaws common at that time.

"Don't let him in," whispered the old lady. "It's nobody means any good to us." But her husband, less suspicious than herself, had already opened the door. A tall, dignified, gentlemanly-looking personage, wrapped in a great coat, thoroughly drenched with rain, walked in and gracefully saluted the old couple.

"Ha, a bad night this, sir," said the aged farmer, impressed with the stranger's bearing. "Throw off your surtout, and take a chair."

"If you please, I will first see that my horse is made comfortable," said the stranger courteously.

"I will see to that, sir," said the farmer, and he conducted his guest into the kitchen, where he had so recently been sitting with his wife. The good woman was not particularly pleased. She had her reasons. Robberies had been committed in the neighborhood, and rumors were about that the rogues who did the mischief were, some of them, provokingly well-dressed and polite. She kept her seat and made not the least movement to provide the new comer any refreshments.

When the farmer returned from the barn, where he had furnished a bountiful repast and a good bed for the horse, he gently reproved his wife for her lack of hospitality, and signified his wish that she should do something for the stranger's comfort. With commendable obedience the dame set about preparing a supper while her husband begged his guest to avail himself of the fire, and dry off the effects of the storm.

Soon after the stranger had finished his supper, the old man informed him that it was usual for him and his wife to have prayers at that hour, and said he, "If you've no objections, sir, we'd be glad for you to join us." The stranger seemed pleased with the proposal.

"Certainly. It will afford me great satisfaction," he said. "Communion with the Divine Being is eminently fit and profitable at the close of the day. Nothing is more important or more rational for man than the habit of devotion."

These remarks, and the grave and serious manner in which they were uttered, completely quieted the apprehensions and disarmed the dislike of the old lady, and increased the courage of the aged host to conduct the service in the presence of one whom he evidently believed to be his superior.

Family worship over, the farmer lighted the gentleman to his chamber, and bidding him good-night, left him to find the repose which he so greatly needed.

"John," said the old lady in a low voice as soon as her husband returned to the kitchen, "do ye s'pose that man means what he says? He talks dreadful good, don't he?"

"Aye, aye, and ain't the look and the way of him good, too? I believe he's got the root o' the matter in him."

"Well, yes, I hope so. But I couldn't a' told it when he come in."

"You a'n't quite so suspicious as you was, eh, goody?"

"I like him better'n I did."

"And do you think you'll lock up your silver spoons, and stick a fork over the door, and sleep with one eye open, eh, goody?" and the old man playfully nudged his wife with his elbow.

"Oh, shut up, John, now," pleaded the old lady — and that was all the defense she attempted to make. She did, in truth, feel a little conscience-stricken for having received her guest so coldly.

While they were about retiring, and the house was still, they thought they heard a sound as of some one talking in the stranger's room. Strong curiosity compelled them to listen. It was the stranger's own voice, and he was engaged in prayer by himself. Silently they crept nearer, and stood on the stairs.

After offering thanks for his preservation from the dangers of the day, and imploring blessings upon the family under that roof, the petitioner continued:

"And now, Almighty Father, if it be thy

holy will, that we shall obtain a name and a place among the nations of the earth, grant that we may be enabled to show our gratitude for thy goodness by our endeavors to fear and obey thee. Bless us with wisdom in our councils, and with success in our battles, and let our victories be tempered with humanity. Endow also our enemies with enlightened minds that they may become sensible of their injustice, and willing to restore liberty and peace. Nevertheless, not my will, but thine be done. Grant the petition of thy servant for the sake of thy beloved Son. Amen."

After that it was evident enough that the good lady of the house did not intend to "sleep with one eye open" from any fears of her guest. If she lay wakeful at all it would be from wondering who in the world that strange man could be. Next morning the gentleman rose early and stated to his host that it was necessary for him to cross the river immediately, at the same time offering to pay for the entertainment of himself and horse. The farmer declined all compensation.

"Well then, sir," continued the stranger, "since you will receive no reward for your trouble, it is but right that you should know who it is on whom you have conferred obligation, and then, perhaps, you will be willing to add to your kindness by aiding me to cross the river. I went out yesterday to obtain some imformation respecting our enemy, and venturing too far, I was surprised by a foraging party, and succeeded in making my escape only by my knowledge of the woods and the swiftness of my horse. My name is George Washington."

The farmer was of course greatly embarrassed and amazed to discover that his guest was so distinguished a person. He urged him to remain long enough to take some breakfast, but Washington excused himself, pleading his earnest desire to cross the river at once. The farmer accordingly called two stout negroes, and then proceeded, leading the horse, towards the water. There, with the assistance of his two men, he succeeded in placing the animal upon a sort of rough raft, and his master taking his place beside him, both were in a short time safely transferred to the other side of the Hudson. When the farmer returned, he was met by the old lady some distance from the house, who seemed to be highly delighted.

"He was a real gentleman," said she, "for after he left the house with you he came back and insisted I should take this," at the same time holding up a handsome present which she had received.

"Do you know, wife, who it was that gave you that?" asked the old man.

"No, sorrer that I don't. Why, *did you find out?*" eagerly.

"That was the 'Commander-in-chief!'" cried the delighted farmer. "It was General George Washington! When I wouldn't take anything from him for keeping him and his horse, he said I ought to know who he was, and then he told me his name.

"Dear me, you don't say!" responded the old lady, with a look of pleased astonishment. "Oh, how sorry I am I didn't know it at the time."

CHAPTER X.

MAC'S ESCAPE.

"Hooraw! Bill McIntyre! Wal, I swan to Columby, — ef you hain't ris from the dead!"

"Bless your happy old soul, Dick Green! *Is that you?*"
And the two brawny Kentuckians, together again after two year's separation, shook and slapped and pawed each other like a pair of great, festive bears.

"Why, old feller," exclaimed Dick, panting with laughter and his antics of rough delight, "I never 'xpected to see you agin. When the red-skins gobbled ye up in that last scrimmage, I said you was a gone goose."

"Haw, haw! good land! So I should a' been ef the Injuns could a' had ther way," interjected Mac. "Trouble was, ye see, they couldn't hold me. I slipped threw ther fingers like a greased pig. Come, let's trade; take a piece o' my bacon, and I'll take a junk o' your hoe-cake."

"Right the fust time, boy! An' now jes' shake out that story. Tell us all how ye did it, — an' whar ye've been sence ye got away — an' what ye're up tew round here. Hev' ye come back to life to jine the army, an' help old Morgan, an' Greene, an' the rest on us whip the Tories? Ha, ha! this is *too* good!"

And with that the two old friends broke into another explosion of laughter, and sat down together on a cotton-wood log.

"Waal," quoth Mac, straightening his jaws into speaking shape, and biting off and swallowing a mouthful of hoe-cake, "sorter, an' sorter not, as ye might say. I've jined the army kinder loose — like the lead on the eend ov a cat-o-nine-tails. I kin dew more execution on the snapper 'n I kin on the stock. That's 'bout the way I fit under Shelby at King's Mountain, fur ye see I got away from the Injuns in good time for that — an' now I'm playin' scout for old Nathan'l."

"So be I!" roared Dick, enthusiastically. "Giv' us yer hand agin! Here, take a swig at my Bets (offering his canteen). But say, Bill, you've got to tell *how ye did it*, right off, now, or ye shan't hev no more hoe-cake."

Bill McIntyre and Dick Green are not mentioned by name in Bancroft's History. But, like thousands of other Revolutionary heroes and patriots, who won only a local fame, these brave "Blue Grass Boys" filled an important place in the great struggle of their time, and nobly deserved their country's gratitude. They belonged to the army, not precisely as regularly enlisted soldiers, but rather as sharpshooters and guerrillas, and ranked among those partisan volunteers who fought for the Whig cause in the great war, and did so much to free the Southern States from British invasion. Their efficiency as scouts procured them frequent appointments in this daring kind of service; and their present meeting is in the border woods between Virginia and North Carolina, looking out for marauding parties of red-coats, whom the famous chase of Cornwallis after Morgan and Greene, in 1781, had let loose upon the settlements.

"Mac" was dressed in a blue linsey-woolsey blouse, or toga, a pair of deer-skin breeches, and a white slouch hat.

Dick wore red small-clothes, an old fatigue jacket of no color, and a militia cap that looked like a battered skillet. Both had knives and pistols in their belts, and carried double-barrelled guns. The fortunes of war that had kept these two friends apart so long had furnished each with plenty of adventures; and the story Dick is just now so eager to hear concerns what happened to Mac when captured by the Indians during Gen. Sullivan's expedition against the Wyoming murderers.

"Waal, comrade," quoth the knight of the leather breeches, speaking with his mouth full, "I've told that little 'xperience o' mine a good many times, but it's new to you, an' as soon 's I kin stay my stomach I'll begin."

"Here, take some o' this cheese, an' then wet down agin. Jerusha! a feller does git powerful hungry an' dry playin' wild-cat in this way."

"Dick," said McIntyre, presently, slapping his companion on the knee, and working down his throat the last of the hoe-cake and bacon, "d'ye ever know how 't feels to hav' all yer fightin' weap'ns stole, an' be tied up, an' druv off, like a slave to a whippin'?"

"I reckon p'raps — but your story comes fust," replied Dick.

"Waal, ye see, them vagabones wouldn't a' nabbed me alive (and Mac took a long pull at the canteen) if an ugly thump on the head with a tommyhawk hadn't sorter stunted me. Howsomever, as 't was, I was in the bilboes 'fore I really knowed it, an' they'd corded my arms like a trussed turkey. Then they snaked me through the woods and over the hills for a couple o' whole days, till they thought the 'pale-faces' couldn't find 'em, an' finally they stopped in a holler between high rocks. The rocks was on three sides, tew hundred foot (or more) up, an' the only open was towards the way we'd come. By that time, I tell ye, my wind was about gin out — they'd tramped so all-fired fast, yer know — an' I reckon the ole red divils themselves thought ther shanks needed some rest. An Injun can't run forever, enny more'n we can. Waal, as I was sayin', they come to a halt, an sot down to breathe an' take somethin'. They felt o' me, an' concluded to loosen the cords on my arms a little. The bloody whelps wanted me to live, so they could tortur' me when they got back to ther tribe. But I tell ye, Dick Green, ef my dander warn't up, you may call me a peep-frog. An old fighter like me snared alive, an' handled like a picked gander! 'Twarn't in natur to stan' it. Oh, thinks I ef I could only git a single free hand!

"Waal, I kep workin' my arms on the sly, an' I found that by a good deal o' squirmin' an' twistin' an' screwin' and pullin' I could draw one hand eeny most out. But I jes' laid low an' showed nothin'. Thinks I to myself, 'Mac, your time'll come — then *start!*' I kep' my eyes open, an' noticed pertiklerly whar they put ther guns, for I thought I might want 'em 'fore mornin'. The savages eat some jerked meat, and drinked some rum, an' as soon 's 'twas dark they got into a circle round me, an' lay down to sleep. I now began to fix my plan. I know'd if I slipped off, leavin' 'em asleep, they'd find my trail, an' besides I knowed 't every one o' them Cherry Valley butchers oughter die. That plan wouldn't do. Then I thought I'd tommyhawk 'em where they lay; but I wan't sure I could dew it quick enough. By the time I settled the fust

— whoop! all the rest on 'em might be on ther feet — an' that ud' be several too many to once."

"How many was thar, Mac?" inquired Dick, who was listening with deep attention.

"Five," said Mac, "an' ye see they was all big fellers, an' I didn't care to fite more'n two or three on 'em at a time. So I lay thar thinkin' an' thinkin'; an' I finally made up my mind that my surest holt 'ud be to git the villains' muskets inter my hands quiet like, an' see if I couldn't use 'em somehow so 's to count the odds agin ther owners. Waal, bimeby the Injuns began to snore, an' then I peeks up my head softly, an' looks round. Thar was a comb o' rock clus by, about breast high, an' a place behind it. Now, says I to myself, 'If I can only pint two o' them iron sojers right at the heads o' two savages to once, so 's to *hit* '*em*, an' hev t'other three guns handy, to use when the rest git up to see what 's the matter, I can fix 'em all.' So I begun to tug at my cords, an' arter a few hard squirms I worked my hands out o' the cords, tho' 't was a plaguey sore job. Then I crep' along on my hands and knees, still 's a catamount, till I got whar the muskets was. I tried 'em all, to see ef they was loaded an' well primed, an' then I carried 'em all behind the rock, an' set three on 'em up thar side by side in sech a way that I could grab 'em on pretty short notice. All this took a good deal o' time, ye know, for I had to move despert slow an' keerful. But I rested a few minnits now to make sure I warn't narvous, an' to watch the red-skins' breathin; then I goes to work, an' fixes t'other two muskets in the shape I want 'em. Fust, I cocked the guns, an' laid 'em across the rock. Then I sighted 'em so to cover the heads o' two Injuns true as a stroke o' lightnin'. I got the guns aimed, and managed to prop 'em so they'd stay aimed, for ye see I meant to pull 'em off both together. Thar was just moonshine enough to draw a bead by, an' it's well thar was, for 'twouldn't do to make any mistakes. When everything was ready I stopped agin, an' waited a little while to stiddy my narves. Then I slid my hands up keerful an' firm — finger on trigger right an' left — then *pulled!* Whang! whang! Both guns spoke the same second. The bullets did ther dooty, an' two big savages sprawled out dead. You oughter seen them other three prance up int' the air, tho', an' yell! Jehu! they beat Bedlam let loose! They made a rush for ther muskits, but the muskits warn't thar. *I had 'em!* An' while they was a starin' an' wonderin' for the missin' weep'ns, I got in two more shots, that killed one an' mort'lly wounded another — so thar was only a single Injun left; and he'd seen enough by that time to make him conclude 'twarn't any place for him. I tell ye what, Dick, the way he lit out from thar, an' shook the dead leaves from his heels, was a lesson to a race-horse. The poor divil run 's ef the ghosts o' all Wyoming and Cherry Valley was arter him."

"Good. What did you do next, Mac?" asked Dick, laughing.

"I chased the feller a little ways, hootin' like a demon, to put a little more skeer into him; then I went back an' took my pick o' the guns, an' what plunder an' rations I could carry, an' struck a bee-line for the Alleghany River."

"Wal, old boy, here ye are all right agin'. Now wet yer whistle — an' confusion to all the country's enemies! That's a capital story o' yourn, Mac, but hang me if I don't b'leeve I kin match it."

"Ten to one ye kin — haw, haw! It's your turn now, Dick."

"I reckon ye never heerd about that trick o' mine at Fort Plain last year — when the Injuns got me, an' I slipped out o' sight on 'em so quick they half believed Belzebub had swaller'd me."

"'*Twarn't* Belzebub, was it?" said Mac.

"No," quoth Dick, "but I was nigh about roasted, for all that."

"Waal, let's have the story."

CHAPTER XI.

HIDE-AND-SEEK WITH THE RED-SKINS.

"'Fore I commence," said Dick, "you'll excuse me if I make one remark. If there's one thing meaner'n another in all't the British 'av did sence they come over here, it's the hirin' o' them Canada an' York State Injuns to help 'em. When they got so low that they had to call on a lot o' greasy, lousy, sneakin' blood-lovin' red niggers to do the butcherin' an' burnin' that they dassn't do themselves, it was time to take their hats an' go home. Them's my sentiments — all which is r'spec'fully s'bmitted — an' now I've relieved my mind.

"Wal, when I was out scoutin' for the garrison at Fort Plain, our party divided up one day, for the enemy'd put us off the scent, an' we thought we could git an inklin' quicker o' what they was tryin' to do, if we spread out over more ground. A couple crossed over, tother side o' the Mohawk, one struck off by the way o' Cobb's Gap, I was to beat round Wilderness Branch, an' the rest went somewhere else. I hadn't ben more'n an hour an' a half reconnoiterin', when all of a sudden, right in the lonesomest part o' the woods, I heered a gun go off, an' a yell *in three different places* that lifted every har on my skin. 'Grate Columby!' thinks I, 'that's Injuns — *be I surrounded* — that's what I want to know?' 'Twan't no time t' ask questions, but in the next breath I did a powerful deal o' lookin', an' quicker'n you could whistle twice I got the hang o' the sitooation. As nigh's I could count in a short second thar was six red niggers arter me, an' one big blaggard whiter'n the rest, that looked like a half-breed, an' he was leadin' 'em on. They hedn't s'rrounded me, an' now 't they'd showed ther hands I didn't mean't they should. My chances looked streaked, though, I'm free to say — seven agin one. Thar wan't one o' them hootin' varmints thet was forty rod off, an' the nighest on 'em was less'n twenty rod. He was the mongrel I spoke on, thet 'pear'd to be chief o' the gang, an' 'twas this one fired the shot. The big scamp was dead sure he'd pepper'd me, or he wouldn't a holler'd.

"Wal, thar didn't seem to be nothin' for me now but to sell my life as dear's I could. Ye see, I'd took care to put myself, whar I show'd less, when the alarm come — an' I wan't long about it nuther. Cover'd betwixt a couple o' trees I brought old Settledog to my cheek (I never'll find the like o' that gun agin, Mac) an' trained it as nigh's I could on the place whar that half-breed rascal was skulked, loadin' his firelock. The rest o' the crew was dodgin' round to get nearer, but I wanted to kill *him* fust. I waited. Time was gittin' precious. I see a skull-feather poke up, an' know'd thar was my man. I see him pint out his gun. Soon's he showed enough o' his face to lay his eye on the britch I pulled trigger, an' old Settledog spoke. Thar was another yell, but thar warn't much war-whoop in it. It was the death-screetch o' the half-breed — an' thar the hulkin' villain lay, pinned through the brain."

"That shot made the red niggers cautious — luckily for me, for I got time to reload. I was mighty near kindom-come, though, that minute, for jes' as I was shettin' down my primin'-pan a savage who'd sneaked round to the wind'ard o' my cover, an' got a sight, fired and snipped off a button o' my jacket. Quick as lightnin' I spotted him behind his gun-smoke, an' drawed on him — an' old Settledog dropped *him* too. Thar was five left o' the red niggers now. But they know'd 'xactly whar I was, ye see, an' bein' in range by this time they all hed ther guns ready. Thinks I, 'If they'll only 'low me to load!'

"Aha, no ye don't, Dick Green! I hedn't fairly got out my powder-plug when on they come. 'Hoo-oo-yi, yi, yi, yi,' an' tommyhawks a swingin'. Two deaths made 'em 'vengeful arter my scalp — an' the sneakinest varmints in the world ain't afraid of an empty gun, ye know. Wal, when I see the hull crew comin' I broke an' run. I had my pistol in my belt, but what was the use o' that just then? I measured my long legs through them woods on 'bout as lively an elk trot as ever took a critter down hill. I know'd I could keep my distance, savin' I didn't get hit — an', I tell ye, *I went*. Bang, said one gun, an' I heered the bullet go, zip! right by my ear. I wonder'd whar the next one 'ud go. Every few minutes I'd dodge one eye over my shoulder to see 'f they was all foller-in'. Bang, went another gun, but thar was no hurt done. On I went, an' on come all the Injuns, yellin' like wolves, an' poppin' their guns arter me as they got a chance. I'd kep' count, ye see, an' they'd fired away at me till I actooally counted the fifth gun — an' I know'd ther hedn't one on 'em stopped to load. The fools hed emptied all ther guns! I couldn't hardly help laffin' — for none o' the shots hed hit me, savin' one 't whistled through my cap, an' one that cut the inside o' my left arm. Ye see I'd zig-zagged a good deal in my runnin', an' kep' the trees betwixt us. Wal, I looked over my shoulder agin, and noticed one savage consid'- able ahead o' the rest. 'Now,' says I, 'old pistol, now's yer chance — an' I whipt the weapon sud- dent out o' my belt, an' wheeled, an' stood stock still. The head Injun' didn't stop (an' maybe he couldn't) till he come inter neat range; an' I shot him dead thar in his tracks.

"Laws, but how 'stonished them red niggers was! In a jiff every scamp on 'em was behind a tree. I got a chance to load old Settledog now. An' the Injuns they improved the time too. So the fight begun agin. Arter that it was shoot an' run, an' run an' shoot — an' shoot an' dodge an' load an' run. I'd ben head- in' for the Fort, an' I'd run a'ready three o' the five mile I hed to go. When I see 't my hand warn't stiddy, an' I didn't make Settledog kill every time, I begun to weaken a little. Ye see, I was pretty well blowed. I could see blood on one o' the red niggers, but none o' the four was disabled. Thinks I, 'Dick, this ain't agoin' to do.' An' jes' as I thought that, a bullet struck my shoulder an' lamed it — an' right then, 's if that warn't bad luck enough, my foot slipped (the ground was gittin' horrid rough) and I tumbled down a gulley, lickety-smash, droppin' old Settledog out o' my hands!

"That was the time I thought I'd lost my scalp sartin sure. I was 'bout used up when I teched bottom in that holler, for the fall banged me bad, besides hurtin' my shoulder so 't I felt faint. It was a queer chance that saved me. Right thar 't the foot o' the ledge, not more'n a yard from whar I struck, lay a grate tree that 'd blowed down, or keeled over itself, some time or 'nuther; an' quick as I looked at it I see 'twas holler. I warn't no very long while gittin' my head inside o' that old tree, and drawin' my legs in arter it, I'll bet a shillin'. Wal, I'd skeersly stowed myself when the red niggers was all at the top o' the gulley, hootin'. Down they come, an' I'll warr'nt every dog on 'em had his scalpin' knife out. I could hear 'em scratchin' an' jumpin' closter'n closter, and when one Injun lit right on top o' my log I felt the goose-pimples rise all over me. They yelped, an' gabbled, an' grunted, an' marvelled this way an' that an' t'otner — an' I knowed by ther tearin' roun't they hedn't seen nothin'. So I lay's quiet's I could, though I warn't extra easy. Wal, them red niggers sarched an' ranted up an' down that are gulley for a haf an hour (so the time seemed to *me*) till I heered one on 'em whoop out, an' they all got together and stood still. I 'xpect that was when they picked up my old Settledog. I vum, Mac, ef I hadn't been hurt I could a' crawled out o' my hole an' fit 'em single-handed ruther t' hed the lousy scamps git that gun. Pretty soon arter that they come round agin —

an' what does they do, all four on 'em, but set down right down on top o' my log.

"Wal, they sot thar, grumblin', an' gabblin' an' gruntin' wi' ther heathen talk, till I thought they never'd git through. Once or twice I could hear 'em say 'Hobommok.' I knowed that was the Injun word for Old Nick — an' I concluded they'd found a way ov 'countin' for whar I'd gone to. Bimeby one or two on 'em got up, an' I heered 'em breakin' up sticks. Then arter a few minutes I smelt smoke. 'Grate Columby!' thinks I, 'what now.' The varmints hed built a fire right agin the log whar I lay!"

"They thought 'twould make a good back-log," said Mac, laughing.

"P'raps they did, but *I* didn't," said Dick. "An' when the log got hot, an' sizzled, an' the funk and fume come pourin' through the knot-holes an' worm-holes, I felt like a live eel hung up in a smoke-house. The heat burnt me, an' the smoke choked me, an' what to do I didn't know. I'd a' gin a fortin to cough an' sneeze jist once, but I knowed 'twas death to do that, anyhow. So I shet my eyes an' swallered, an' bor' it like a martyr. An' that warn't the wust o' my sufferin', for at fust I couldn't help horribly mistrustin' that the divils hed guessed out my trick, an' meant to burn me in my hole. But I found arterwards they was only roastin' some squirrels, thet I 'spose some one or t'other on 'em had in his pouch.

"Finally they got ther cookin' done, an' let the fire go out, an' I could breath agin. But the old log was hot, an' I could feel myself sizzle long arter the las' spark was gone. Zounds, Mac, *I can feel it now!* The soak o' sweat, an' the smart o' the roastin't I got in that old holler tree, come back fresh every time I tell on't. Wal, the Injuns et ther dinner, an' then went to smokin' ther pipes! Thar I lay still as a dead bear, achin', and sufferin', an' wonderin' in my soul 'f they never'd go. Sometimes I could hear them heathens walkin' round, an' sometimes I knowed they was settin' on the log. Ugh! It makes me squirm to think what tough waitin' that was! It 'peared to me three or four hours 'fore them blasted red niggers finally cleared out — an' even then I couldn't be sartin they'd all gone till I'd waited an' harked a good while longer. But when I couldn't hear nothin' more, an' concluded thar warn't nothin' more to hear, I let myself out of that log, like a snake crawlin' out o' his skin; and found the coast clear. I felt pretty skakey, but I sarched round sometime for old Settledog 'fore I went. 'Twan't no use, though. Beyend doubt the Injuns hed stole it. So I turned my toes towards Fort Plain, an' by sundown I was among friends."

"That *was* a lucky escape — an' a narrer one — wan't it, Dick!" quoth Mac reflectively.

"You're right. An' now I vote thet we both turn our toes to headquarters. We shan't find no red-coats' trail round here, I reckon. Come Mac."

After looking at the priming of their guns, and picking their flints, so as to be prepared for any sudden emergency, the two comrades rose and made their way to camp.

CHAPTER XII.

KING'S MOUNTAIN.

"Then *you* were there, helping fight the British Major, eh, Cæsar?" asked Mr. Pinckney, of an old, shrewd house-slave, as he was talking with him one day about the battles in South Carolina.

"*Wus I dar?* Guess I warn't nowhar else, on ole King's-Mountain day."

"Then you know what were the dispositions of the two armies on that memorable occasion?"

"Disp'sition? Yah. De disp'sition of de red-coats wuz to whip us, and our disp'sition wuz not to let 'em. He! he! he!"

"No, no, you don't understand me, Cæsar. I mean in what manner or order was the attack made; where were the different American captains, with their several companies, stationed?"

Cæsar scratched his head and considered, and finally referred the question to "Sarjint Homes," who luckily happened along. "He wuz dar, an' he kin 'scribe dat battle better 'an me."

"Well, Sergeant, I should be happy to have a narrative of that affair, and as you were in it you can relate it correctly."

Sergeant Homes cheerfully complied with Mr. Pinckney's request, and as he began his story, old Cæsar stood by to vouch for the facts, and add characteristic comments of his own.

"Major Ferguson, with a force of eleven hundred British soldiers, was encamped on King's Mountain. The chief business of these heroes was to range through the northern part of the State, and steal all the cattle, sheep and provisions they could find, to supply Cornwallis' army with food."

"Dat's true!" put in Cæsar. "Golly! warn't we mad when dey druv off Massa Samuel's best cow!"

"We concluded to stop their thieving," continued the sergeant, "so we collected a little army, of about nine hundred men, and started out to give them a lesson. We chose a good time, and found them all in quarters, on the mountain-top. Just before we arrived there, we captured an express, who was carrying dispatches from Ferguson to Cornwallis. We opened the dispatches, and read them aloud at the head of the line. In them he said, 'I hold a position on the King's Mountain that all the Whigs and rebels out of jail cannot take.'

"The 'Whigs and rebels' received this with 'three groans,' and very soon the word of command went round, 'Pick your flints! prime fresh! All ready to fight!'"

"Yah, yah!" chuckled old Cæsar, "an' dey all minded dat order de fus' time. I 'member how Massa Samuel, an' de res' uv 'em, picked an' packed, an' got up an' got!"

"We passed on quickly, till we reached the base of the mountain," continued the sergeant. "Then we were divided into three companies or divisions, so as to ascend on different sides of the mountain at once, and surround them on the top as we came together. When Colonel Sevier's column was seen on the right, steadily advancing, the British came down upon them with great fury in a regular charge. Sevier's men did nobly, but they could not resist such a terrible avalanche of bayonets and balls. Before they were completely routed, however, our division under Cleaveland and Williams appeared on the left and poured such a storm into the British ranks that they were obliged to relinquish the pursuit of Sevier, and fall back on the defensive.

"Meeting Cleaveland's column at an advantage, they succeeded in driving them down the hill; but by that time Sevier's men had recovered, and returned to the fight. These galled the enemy so severely in their turn, that they gave up the chase of Cleaveland, and wheeled upon their first antagonists. Receiving reinforcements from within the lines, the British made their next charge against our centre, under Campbell and Shelby, and drove them nearly to the bottom of the hill. But now the right and left columns of the Americans had rallied, and come back to the encounter, maddened by the loss of so many of their brave comrades, and determined to avenge their death. The British, finding themselves attacked in flank and rear, relinquished the pursuit of Campbell and Shelby, and attempted to reascend the hill. They found it bloody work. Murderous volleys poured in upon them, from the right and left, so that death met them at every step. When Campbell and Shelby heard the roar of musketry upon both flanks of the enemy, they supposed the British were retreating, and turned themselves to pursue, with loud shouts of victory. But the enemy were not yet conquered. They gathered all their force, and made one more desperate charge. But it was all in vain. The Americans now stood their ground, and not only that, they pushed the British so sorely as to force them into their encampment. Then came the fiercest struggle of the day. The British were completely hemmed in on all sides. With bayonets, and with butcher-knives fastened to their guns, they charged upon this narrowing circle of patriots with the energy of despair. But the Americans loaded rapidly and aimed deliberately, each marksman bringing down his victim at nearly every discharge."

"Dat's so," chimed in old Cæsar. "When we penned 'em in dar, I picked out an ossifer, an' whop! He dropped, an' nebber knowed what hurt him."

"While the battle raged at this fearful rate," continued the sergeant, "and the enemy were rapidly getting the worst of it, we heard the English commander order his soldiers to mount, and crush the rebels. There was a pause of a moment. Instead of the roar of musketry, the ominous click of the gun-locks spoke, in sign that brave hearts were waiting for the worst to come. The next instant Ferguson and Dupoistre, with their whole force of British horse and foot, burst like an avalanche down the mountain's side.

"But every American rifle was loaded, and almost before the enemy were fairly out of their entrenchments, a stream of fiery death met them full in their faces. Ferguson was in front, and fell at the first discharge, with seven mortal wounds. Dupoistre's regulars came down fiercely with bayonets and sabres, but even more fiercely the patriots met the shock of the onset. Not Agincourt nor Cressy, nor the bloodiest field in chivalric history, remembers a more terrible clash of arms. Had the heavens rained British bayonets, our determined troops would not have given way. Like lions they rushed to the carnage; like martyrs they went to the death. Officers and soldiers together, with bloodshot eyes and parched tongues, faced the headlong foe. Whig and Tory fought foot to foot, and felt the hot panting of each other's breath.

"It was an awful struggle. The tide of battle ebbed and flowed in blood. The fate of the day hung in even balance — and then it turned. The hands of Freedom had dealt the heaviest blows. A cry for quarter was heard, and the Tory ranks showed the white flag. Victory! victory! The enemy threw down their arms, and patriot troops were once more conquerors!

"Of the over eleven hundred British and Tories, two hundred and forty were killed, and two hundred wounded. More than seven hundred were taken prisoners of war, with all their arms and ammunition. Not one of them escaped. As they composed about one fourth of the army of Cornwallis, their capture was a severe blow to the British army in the South."

"Yah," added old Cæsar, "an' I reckon it stopped all dere cattle-stealin', too."

"You think it served them right, do you?" said Mr. Pinckney.

"Sarve 'em right, Massa Pinckney? Yah! Red-coats no bizness yere, anyhow, stealin' tings, an' shootin' men-folks — an' talkin' sassy to de wimmin! Ugh! Glad um gone! We no want 'em."

CHAPTER XIII.

MAD ANTONY.

THE following letter, from a young volunteer in the American army to his mother at home, gives a graphic description of one of the most gallant and thrilling engagements in the whole war of the Revolution.

The scene of the battle — which was Gen. Wayne's most brilliant exploit, and helped to give him the epithet of "Mad Antony" for his dashing bravery — was near the Hudson River, forty-two miles north of New York.

"IN CAMP, STONY POINT, July 17, 1779.
"DEAR MOTHER:
"I AM well enough to write, though

a wound in my left shoulder reminds me that something has happened, and that it's a wonder I'm alive.

We had a fearful time night before last storming the old Fort here. It was by all odds the most terrible fight I've been in since I enlisted. You know the British took the fort on Stony Point from us. Well, General Washington was determined to get it back again. So what does he do but order General Wayne to undertake the job. He was just the man for the work, for he's keen and shrewd as a fox, and bold as a lion. You ought to see him in a battle once! He'll face anything — and there can't be a coward in the ranks when 'Mad Antony' leads. I don't believe Old Nick himself would stop him, or his soldiers, when he's fairly started on a charge.

"After marching fourteen miles over mountains, across gullies and through muddy swamps, we came in sight of the fort about eight o'clock in the evening. It was a hard march, and we were tired. But the worst was to come.

"General Wayne divided his little army into two divisions, so that they could attack the fort on opposite sides at the same time. In front of each of these divisions was a van-guard of a hundred and fifty men, all volunteers, and in front of each van-guard was a skirmisher squad of twenty men. They were to go ahead and clear the ground for the others, by tearing down the tree-fences, brush and rubbish which the enemy had piled up to stop the way.

"One of these advance companies was under the command of Col. Fleury, and the other was led by Major Posey. When everything was ready we commenced marching towards the fort. It was situated on high land and was well protected with walls, abattis, and deep trenches filled with water. We started about half past eleven. As everything was to be done with the point of the bayonet, we weren't allowed to load our guns. The order was to march with empty muskets; not to speak a word; make no noise — and not a man dodge or run, under pain of death! The officers gave all their commands in whispers.

"By good luck we had found a black fellow who sold strawberries at the fort, and knew the countersign, which, curiously enough, happened to be, that night, '*The fort is ours.*' Well, this black fellow was sent ahead of the skirmishers, along the causeway that led over the flooded marsh at the foot of the hill. The outpost sentry on guard there received the countersign all right, and while he stood talking with the darkey two of our men suddenly grabbed and gagged him. So we all marched without a challenge over the causeway to the bottom of the hill under the fort. Everything was as still as death. Our officers formed us according to the plan, and we began to go up the hill, one division on one side, and one on the other. Moving silent and cautious, we reached the next sentry line, and then crack went a picket gun — and away on the left, crack! went another. Seeing we were discovered, we pushed forwards at double quick, and now we could hear the ringing voice of General Wayne cheering and urging on his men — for it was no use to keep still any longer. The whole garrison was up, and the terrible work begun. Oh, how the ramparts blazed, and how the bullets whistled among us in the dark! The limbs of the trees cracked: the men shouted; the wounded groaned and fell. But we rushed on, for 'Mad Antony' put courage into us. Our advance runners tore away obstructions and pulled down barricades. On we rushed through the abattis and up to the intrenchments. We clambered swiftly on the ramparts and drove the Red-coats in at the point of the bayonet, they shooting down our men every minute as they gave back, and disputing every inch of ground. General Wayne was wounded in the head and fell, but he soon staggered up, and resting on one knee

Capture of Stony Point. Page 144.

shouted, 'Forward men! carry me into the fort! I'll die at the head of my column!' I was near him, so I helped two or three others carry him in. Our men had fought their way into the center of the fort, and there we met Col. Fleury's division which had come up on the other side. Gen. Wayne's plan had worked perfectly, and not a single movement had failed. Fleury struck the British flag with his own hands, and hoisted ours in its place. Then the enemy surrended — though 'twas like pulling teeth to own they'd been beaten. When we found that the fort was really ours, I tell you, mother, we hollered and yelled and shouted loud enough to be heard half way down to New York.

"Out of our eight hundred we had fifteen killed and eighty-three wounded. The enemy had sixty-three killed. We took several cannons, and mortars, a great many muskets, shells, shot and tents, and about five hundred and fifty prisoners. We call it a splendid victory. We are going to blow up the fort and destroy all the defences, so that it shall be of no more use to the British.

"Don't feel anxious about my wound, for it's a slight one, and I shall soon be round again. So will 'Mad Antony.'

"From Your affectionate Son,

" ———— "

So important was the capture of Stony Point regarded by Congress, and so highly did they estimate the heroism of the officers, that they ordered three emblematical medals to be prepared and given respectively to General Wayne, Colonel Fleury, and Colonel Stewart.

In addition to this, Wayne received the most flattering commendations from numerous gentlemen, eminent for their intelligence and position both in civil and military life. In fact, Benjamin Rush wrote to him, saying: —

"There was but one thing wanting in the

result of your late attack upon Stony Point to complete your happiness; and that is, the wound you received should have affected your hearing; for I fear you will be stunned through those organs with your own praises."

CHAPTER XIV.

WASHINGTON'S STRATAGEM.

On the fourth of July, 1856, a gentleman and his wife were stopping at Yonkers, New York, a romantic town on the eastern bank of the beautiful Hudson. They had attended a juvenile celebration held in honor of the day, and, returning from this, had accepted an invitation to visit an old, colonial mansion that stood near the river. This house was surrounded by rows of noble trees, like tall, military sentinels set to protect it, and between the openings of their shade beautiful gardens and smooth, green lawns stretched away on different sides, smiling in the sun. The beds and walks were free from weeds, and neatly trimmed, giving evidence of the constant vigilance and care bestowed upon them, and the borders of shiny, wax-leaved box, seemed the thrifty growth of many years. As the couple strolled about the grounds, the guide who accompanied them and pointed out the historic localities, told them an interesting tradition, connected with the mansion itself.

"Did you say that General Washington once used to visit here?" asked the lady.

"I did, madam. Washington had his head-quarters some miles further up the river, but it is said that he and the family residing here were old acquaintances, and being much attached to them, and charmed by the rare social attractions at the mansion, the tired warrior loved to come here for an hour of recreation, as often as his pressing duties would allow.

"The father of this family seemed to feel the warmest personal friendship for Washington, and though he assumed no active part in the war, he either professed sympathy for the patriot cause, or declared himself strictly a conscientions neutral. His treatment of the general was always marked by affectionate cordiality, and the courtesy of an old-fashioned gentleman."

"At that time were the British stationed anywhere very near this place?" asked the gentleman.

"Not *very* near, and still not so very far away. This was the border-land between the two armies. The Americans were up the river, at and around West Point, and the British were below. Each party, therefore, could make excursions into this part of the country. Well, to come to the tradition, as I have heard it related:

"On one occasion, Washington was invited to dine at this house on a particular day and hour; and the invitation was pressed with such earnestness as to arouse the suspicions of the American commander, that some special design was concealed under it. These suspicions were greatly increased when the master of the mansion intimated to him that his habit of bringing a guard with him when he came here was a useless precaution, and seemed to imply a want of confidence in the good faith of his host; and expressed the hope that he would come the next time unattended.

"Pondering over this singular request, and connecting it with the man's anxious manner, Washington finally could not help believing that some treachery was intended. He accepted the invitation, but at the same time determined to plan his visit in such a way as to defeat any villainy which might be meditated. The time fixed upon for the dinner was two o'clock; but Washington arrived an hour before the time.

"After the usual greetings and courtesies were passed, the host led his distinguished visitor to the piazza for a sociable walk. The quick eye of the general soon discovered an unusual nervous restlessness in his companion's manner, not at all consistent with tranquility of mind. Why was the man so preoccupied and absent — so full of starts and incoherencies? Why did he every now and then cast furtive glances in a certain direction? A variety of close questions and keen remarks on the part of the general, uttered, however, as if they were purely incidental, plainly increased this appearance of agitation. Washington noticed, too, that the man quailed as often as he caught his eye. He was now more than ever convinced that his professed friend was a traitor, and had plotted some perfidy against him. As yet there was no *proof*, but that was only a question of time — and he longed for the time to come. Presently the distant clatter of horses' feet was heard, and the eyes of both the men turned in the direction of the sound.

"Just over the brow of that hill (and the guide pointed to an eminence a short distance away), they saw a company of dragoons coming down the road on a brisk trot."

"Were they British or Americans?" asked the lady.

"They were dragoons in British uniforms."

"O, dear!" replied the lady. "And *how did* Washington escape?"

"I will tell you," answered the guide. "The horsemen quickened their pace, as they approached the house, and they rode at a full gallop straight towards the piazza where the two men stood.

"'Bless me!' exclaimed Washington, 'what cavalry are these coming so near?'

"'A party of British light horse,' replied his host, 'who are sent here for my protection.'

"Doubtless the traitor felt greatly relieved now that his plot seemed about to be consummated.

"'British horse sent here while I am your guest?' said Washington, with a sternness and startling emphasis which made the other recoil before him.

"'What does this mean, sir?' added Washington, with increased energy. During this short colloquy, the soldiers had reined up at the gate, and began to dismount. The perfidious host, supposing that these horsemen were, of course, his party, in the moment of his hasty triumph, exposed himself. He familiarly approached Washington, and laying his hand upon his shoulder, said to him, 'General, *you are my pris'ner!*'

"That was the crowning part of the plot this disguised Tory had been playing — and with (as he now believed) such perfect success. The American commander was trapped — betrayed into British hands. His escape seemed impossible.

"Never was man more completely mistaken. As he uttered the words 'You are my prisoner,' Washington, instead of exhibiting the least alarm, calmly replied, 'I think not, but, sir, I know that *you are mine*. Officer, *arrest this traitor!*'

"Imagine the astonishment of the treacherous Tory, when he saw the 'British' officer, instead of seizing the American general, proceed immediately to obey his orders! Before he could recover from his amazement, he found *himself* a pinioned prisoner in the hands of the soldiers. He then learned, to his terrible chagrin, that these dragoons were *American soldiers in British uniforms!*

"It seems that Washington, in order to satisfy himself whether his suspicions were correct, had ordered a company of his own soldiers to disguise themselves in this manner, and appear at the mansion punctually at a quarter before two o'clock. As we have seen, Washington's suspicions proved to be well founded. The false friend, outwitted by his intended victim, had been caught in his own trap; and now nothing remained for him but to follow his captors to the American camp, and expect the fate of a traitor."

"Did the man ever make any confession?" asked the gentleman.

"Yes," replied the guide. "He confessed that he had been offered a large sum of money, if he would betray Washington into the power of the British, and at two o'clock the house was to have been surrounded by a party of the king's troops, sent to make the general a prisoner."

"A very narrow escape!" said the gentleman.

"Yes, and the traitor deserved hanging, as much as if he hadn't failed," said the guide. "The will was as bad as the deed, to my thinking."

"What was done with him?" asked the lady.

"Not much of anything, madam. Washington at first intended to make him suffer severely, but the man's family and friends interceded so powerfully that he finally decided not to proceed to extremes. He kept him a while in prison, and then pardoned him, and sent him home."

CHAPTER XV.

AN ARMY CAUGHT NAPPING.

On the 24th of December, 1776, two ragged but brave-hearted American soldiers, comrades of the same company, were engaged beside their camp-fire in cleaning their guns preparatory to some important service.

"I tell ye what, Zeb," said one, "that scratch on Long Island was a bad affair for our side. The old gin'ral was all right, and if he could ha' been everywhere to once, it might 'a turned out different. But, I say, some o' his under officers ought to be cashiered. Why didn't old Sullivan keep that furder pass well guarded? If he had, the British wouldn't uv turned his left and got in his rear. That did the mischief. For wen they got behind us, them Dutchmen was in front, and there we was between two fires. Didn't we run for it? first one way, then t'other, and brought up agin the enemy's fire every time! If we hadn't pitched right through the reg'lar's column, with our lives in our teeth, we'd never found our way to camp agin."

"That's so, Zeke," replied his comrade. "And what a fool old Howe was that he didn't follow up his chance. They might 'a drove us into East River, an' made nigh the hull on us prisoners. But he let nine thousand slip — and here we be. Wall, I'm sorry our friends in the country feel chop-fallen. 'Tain't the wust that ever was. We can't expect to beat every time we fight. We've got to risk the chances of war."

"Tut, tut there, Zeb," said Zeke, with a warning expression in his eye. "Expectin' to get licked sometimes, ain't safe soldiership, to *my* thinkin'. The way is, to go into battle every time, *expectin' to whip!* Then you feel strong enough to do it, and not without. Meet the inimy, and think he's goin' to give you a lickin'! Pooh! no man will fight wuth a fo'pence wi' that kind o' liver in him!"

"Give it up, then, an' p'raps ye're right, comrade," said Zeb. "Still, I don't see why all our friends should be so dumfounded and down in the mouth jist because we've lost one battle."

"It was a great disapp'intment," said Zeke, "but no matter. Perhaps we'll make it all up agin to-morrer."

"Do you know where we're ordered?"

"No, but it's pretty well known t' we're goin' to make an attack somewheres. British ain't lookin' for us, now, ye know."

"Wall, I'll trust old Gin'ral Washington," said Zeb, giving the last rub to his gun-barrel. "If the rest 'll obey his orders, and do their duty, we'll come out ahead, sure."

In the middle of the following night, the two soldiers, with their thousands of comrades, were roused from sleep by the loud drum-roll, and knew that the hour for active duty was at hand.

"Great guns!" shuddered Zeb, as he leaped out of his blanket, "but it's a bitter cold night, though."

"Not only cold," replied Zeke, "but it storms like chain shot. Hear how the hail rattles down on the old tent."

There was no time for comments, however. It was the soldier's business to obey.

In a few minutes, they were standing shoulder to shoulder with their company, ready to march at the word of command.

The object which Washington had in view on this occasion was to attack all the British posts on the Delaware River at the same instant, and thus drive the enemy from New Jersey or take them prisoners of war. By Washington's plan, General Irvine was to cross the river at Trenton Ferry, and take possession of a road just below the town, so as to cut off the escape of the British by the bridge there, or along the shore.

Washington crossing the Delaware.   Page 161.

General Cadwallader was to pass at Dunk's Ferry, and take Mount Holly, then in the possession of the English, whilst Washington himself, assisted by Generals Sullivan and Green, would cross nine miles above Trenton, with four thousand men, and march at once upon the town.

General Irvine attempted to carry out the part assigned him, but the river was so blocked up with ice that he found it impossible to cross. General Cadwallader met with the same difficulty. He succeeded, however, in getting some of his infantry over, but finding it impossible to follow with his artillery, he recalled the infantry, and gave up the effort. Washington himself succeeded, though with great hazard and hardship. Having crossed the river, he divided his force into two divisions. One of these divisions advanced towards Trenton by a road along the shore of the river, and the other marched by the Pennington road. As the distance to Trenton by either of these roads was about the same, both divisions were expected to reach the town at the same time. Washington, therefore, gave orders that each division should attack the outposts of the enemy so soon as they were reached, and drive them in, and then follow closely upon them into the town. Thus the Americans could fall upon the main body of the enemy so suddenly that they would not be able to form for their defence. Zeb and Zeke were in the division under Washington. They suffered extremely with the cold and wet in crossing the river, and we may be sure they found that nine miles' march, from four o'clock in the morning to eight, no children's play. At eight o'clock the report of a musket was heard at the head of the column.

"We've reached 'em!" said Zeke, in a low tone, to his elbow-man.

"Hark!" whispered Zeb, in reply; "there goes a volley. We've come upon the picket-guard."

Rapidly the few words of command ran

through the lines. Every officer was on the alert, and the soldiers pressed forward with quick and resolute step. They all knew their general's plan at last, and felt eager for victory.

"Now we shall have it," said Zeb.

"And we'll give it to 'em," said Zeke.

As the firing increased at the head of the column, the whole division became wonderfully excited. Presently the report of musketry was heard from another point.

"That's t' other division," said Zeb. "They've arriv' just in the nick o' time. I knew they would!"

"Ha!" broke out Zeke, "see that runaway red-coat sentinel firin' from that winder. Lemme pick him off." Zeke levelled his gun and fired.

"There they run; see 'em, see em!" shouted Zeb, taking aim at three or four of the picket guard, who were retreating behind a barn.

In this way the Americans advanced, fired on from windows, and from behind walls and buildings, but with little damage, till the outposts were all passed, and the guards killed or driven in.

Colonel Rawle, a brave British officer, seeing the sentinels retreating, and the Americans advancing, paraded his men, and endeavored to make a stand against the Yankees. But it was of no avail.

"He'll stan' till he falls," muttered Zeke and Zeb, and pointed their muskets at him. Several other soldiers did the same.

Just at that moment a ball struck Colonel Rawle, and he sank, mortally wounded.

"Told you so," continued Zeke. "Them red-coats had better give it up, or they'll all go the same way."

The enemy, seeing their officer fall, and having no hope of resisting successfully the onset of the Americans, commenced filing off to the right, so as to retreat and gain the road to Princeton. The vigilant eye of Washington saw the manœuvre. He immediately ordered a detachment to head them off, whilst he advanced rapidly in pursuit. His object was to surround them.

The plan succeeded. The retreating soldiers, in trying to flee from one portion of the American army, found themselves rushing upon the bayonets of another. Soon they were encompassed on all sides, and, finding retreat in any direction impossible, and the Americans pouring in a fire of musketry upon them from all points, surrendered themselves prisoners of war.

"Hurrah!" shouted Zeke.

"Hurrah!" hallooed Zeb.

"Hurrah!" roared all the American troops.

Green and Sullivan, arriving by the other road, had done prompt and gallant work. All resistance had been overpowered. The artillery of the British had been seized, and the royal army in Trenton was hopelessly demoralized. In a very short time the fighting was over, and victory perched on the patriot banners. About a thousand of the enemy were made prisoners of war. Six excellent brass cannon, twelve hundred small arms, with three standards, besides baggage, etc., were taken by Washington. Five hundred more of the enemy, among whom was a company of cavalry, would also have been taken if General Irvine had succeeded in crossing the river. They escaped by the road which his division should have guarded.

After the battle was over, our two Yankees sat down with their company (in comfortable quarters for the first time in many weeks), and chatted merrily over their breakfast.

"Ah, Zeb, when we got Rawle and his Dutchmen there between our fires, I *knowed* they'd have to s'rrender."

"Well ye might know," quoth Zeb. "Haw, haw! Think this 'll 'bout make up for the bastin' we got on Long Island, hey?"

"Jist about fair an' square. And it 'll make the hull country 'laff an' grow fat," said Zeke. "I tell ye it 'll warm up their hearts like a spring rain. Wonder how many were killed; do you know?"

"There couldn't a' been many; they didn't stan' long enough. I heern Corporal Smike say there was about twenty o' the Hussians killed, and two on our side. Thar was two more o' our poor fellers got froze to death."

General Washington sent the captured Hessians into the interior of Pennsylvania, allowing them to keep their baggage, and gave orders that they should be treated with humanity. Such kindness from a conqueror greatly surprised the Hessians, and awakened in their minds a high degree of veneration for Washington, whom they called a *very good rebel*.

A short time after this successful engagement, which astonished the British as much as it encouraged the Americans, the following quaint and pithy song was sung by the Yankees with great glee.

BATTLE OF TRENTON.

On Christmas-day in seventy-six,
Our ragged troops, with bayonets fixed,
   Their march on Trenton made.
The Del'ware, see! the boats below!
The light obscured by hail and snow!
   But not a man afraid.

We marched to fight the Hessian band,
That dared invade fair freedom's land,
   And quarter in that place.
Great Washington he led us on,
Whose gallant flag, in storm and sun
   Had never known disgrace.

All silently the stream we cross'd,
Pelted with sleet, and numb with frost,
   But eager for the fray.
Greene on the left at six began;
The right was led by Sullivan;
   We marched till dawn of day,

" To arms!" the sunrise terror spread;
" The Yanks are risen from the dead,
   And thundering into town!"
Some scampered here, some scampered there,
They fired their bullets in the air,
   And flung their muskets down.

Twelve hundred fools of British pence,
With all their colors, guns and tents,
  Our trophies were that day.
The frolic o'er, the bright canteen
Went round convivial hands between,
  To drive dull care away.

Now brothers all, ye patriot band,
Sing glad deliverance from the hand
  Of British tyranny.
And as our life is but a span,
We'll kiss the tankard while we can,
  For Trenton's victory.

It is evident, from this song, that teetotalism was not popular at that time, and, unfortunately, it seldom is in camps in time of war.

Several other songs were composed on the same battle. One of them contained a sarcastic stanza on Hessian courage. One of the standards taken from the Hessians bore a Latin motto which signified, "I know no danger," and which was not displayed in the battle where the standards were surrendered. To this boasting motto the following verse refers:

" The man who submits, without striking a blow,
May be said, in a sense, *no danger to know;*
I pray, then, what harm, by the humble submission
At Trenton, was done by the standard of Hessian?"

CHAPTER XVI.

A BOLD MANŒUVRE.

"Well, Zeke, I reckon our work for this campaign ain't done yit. I heern that Cornwallas is in the Jerseys, and if that's so our Gin'ral 'ill be arter him, or I'm no Yankee."

"The sooner the better," replied Zeb, as he stripped off the skin of a coon which he had recently shot. "I should like to see some o' them red-coats shook out o' their shoes, so I might git a pair. But till then I s'pose I shall have to wear this skin on one foot, and shoot another for its mate, if I can. Howsumever, I ought to be thankful, for some of our poor fellers ain't so well off as this."

"I know it," said Zeke. "I wonder what

Congress is thinkin' on that they don't supply the army with clothes. Some o' the troops are 'most naked."

"Yes; and the wust o' the hull on't is bein' without shoes an' stockin's. Walkin' in the snow an' slush, and on the ice, barefoot, ain't no luxury. There's some in our comp'ny now, cut an' froze so bad they leave blood-marks every step they take. If I don't git another coon or skunk skin to make another mocassin, t'will be the same with me."

"Hark! hark! ther's an alarm — we've got to report on duty, barefoot or not."

Both the soldiers rushed to their tents, seized their guns, and ran to their colors. The whole camp was in motion. Drums and trumpets were sounding, and soon the news spread throughout the army that Cornwallis was approaching Trenton, with a large number of troops. Distant reports of muskets were heard. These increased in rapidity, showing that a skirmish had begun between the advance guard of the enemy, and the

American outposts. As the sound continued to come nearer, it became evident that the outposts were being driven in, and in a short time Cornwallis, with his whole army, would be upon them. It was now late in the afternoon, and Washington gave orders for all his troops to retreat across a small stream called the Assumpinck, which ran through the town.

He immediately planted some cannon at favorable points on the bank of this stream, to check the British if they should attempt to follow. Soon the scarlet uniforms of the English were seen approaching. On, on they came, with the evident design of crossing the stream, and attacking the main body of the Americans. They arrived at a fording-place of the Assumpinck, and attempted to cross. But the cannon of the Yankees annoyed them so much at this point that they relinquished the attempt, and tried it at another place. But Washington had anticipated them there, and from another quarter opened on them such a galling fire as induced them to abandon this attempt, also. Finding no place where they could cross without incurring considerable loss, Cornwallis called back his troops, and concluded to give his soldiers a night's rest, with the intention of attacking the Yankees the next day. So the two armies encamped on the opposite sides of the stream, in full sight of each other, expecting bloody work on the morrow.

Washington was now placed in an extremely critical condition. The army of Cornwallis was in every respect superior to his own. Nothing but a narrow, fordable stream separated them. Early to-morrow he would undoubtedly be attacked, and, with his comparatively feeble force, he would probably be defeated, and if so, his army would be likely to be destroyed or taken prisoners. This would leave the whole of New Jersey in the possession of the British; Philadelphia would be open to them. The whole nation would be greatly discouraged, and it would be exceedingly difficult to enlist new troops. He decided that he *could not risk a battle* with any reasonable hope of success. But, on the other hand, if he should attempt to retreat, the enemy would detect the movement too soon. Or, if they did not, by crossing the Delaware, since neither ice nor ferry was now passable, he would probably suffer great loss, if not the entire destruction of his army. *Something*, however, must be done, and done speedily.

Washington, therefore, devised a bold stratagem. Princeton, which was ten miles from Trenton, was in possession of the British. Washington rightly reasoned that as Cornwallis had left there with a larger part of his troops, Princeton could not be very strongly guarded, and therefore, if he could manage to get away without being discovered, he might reach the town, and perhaps capture the troops that held it. He resolved to make the attempt. As soon as it was sufficiently dark for the movement to be made without attracting the attention of the British, all the baggage was silently conveyed to Burlington. About one o'clock in the morning, the camp-fires of the Americans, which had been kept burning all night, were renewed and the sentinels were ordered to march backwards and forwards between them and the British, so that the enemy might receive the impression that nothing unusual was going on in the American camp. After appointing guards at the bridge, and other passes of the narrow stream, Washington secretly drew off his army and marched toward Princeton. Cornwallis knew nothing of this movement, and was greatly surprised and chagrined in the morning, when he found that the Yankees were gone. He at once suspected Washington's object, and therefore immediately set out to prevent its accomplishment, if possible.

Two or three regiments at Princeton had been ordered by Cornwallis to come to him at Trenton. About sunrise Washington met these regiments. An engagement immediately commenced. The American militia, being ahead, were the first to be engaged. Many of them were raw recruits, not accustomed to actual warfare. Their conduct, and the result of this action, and of the attempt on Princeton, may be learned from the following conversation of our two soldiers, which took place at the next night's camp-fire.

"Wall, Zeb, this has been a glorious day for us."

"That's true, but it's been an awful tough one for me, Zeke."

"Guess you're right, Zeb."

"I got it ruther stiff on the road, but you've got a better right to complain than I."

"Complain! Who's said anything about complainin'? But look o' them feet!"

Zeke held up his extremities, with one old, worn-out shoe, that looked as though it had been through a thrashing-machine, and one remnant of a coon-skin moccasin, consisting chiefly of the raw strip that held it round the ankle. Both these wretched relics were stained with blood, for poor Zeke's feet had been terribly cut by his severe march over a frozen road. Carefully making a track on the snow, he left a crimson spot, nearly the size of the sole.

"There, ain't *that* tough?" added he; "and the same to go through to-morrer, and the next day, and the next — and I don't know how long, 'less I can find some shoes here, or hook a pair off some dead Englishman."

"Poor chance for that, Zeke," replied his tent-mate. "Ther's lots of our brave fellers in the same fix, and I guess every red-coat that fell had his shoes or boots tore off'n his feet 's soon's he was down, by them 't wanted 'em more'n he."

"Wall, I don't care," continued the suffering soldier, "we've got another vict'ry, anyhow."

"'Twas a close rub, though, warn't it?"

"Yes."

"Them raw militia didn't stan' up wuth a fo'pence. I'm ashamed on 'em. When they see the British comin', they run like sheep from a strange dog. They like t' upset the rest on us when they rushed back amongst us there, pell-mell. And that ain't the wust on 't; I b'leeve Gin'ral Mercer wouldn't a' got his mortal wound if they hadn't made such cowardly work. He exposed himself to everything, tryin' to rally 'em, and put a little courage into 'em — and it cost him his life."

"And I thought Washington would git shot down, too, for he was dreadfully exposed," said Zeke.

"I know it. But what else could he do? Them militia, who'd never smelt gunpowder afore, were runnin' right down on his division, and there was danger that they'd ketch the panic. So Washington rode right ahead, exposin' himself to the fire of the inimy, and then our reg'-lars were ashamed not to foller where *he* led."

"Sakes! an' how close we pushed! Why, where I was, we got within pistol shot o' the red-coats, 'fore they stopped their firin'. Then we dashed at 'em, an' they begun to run."

"Where d'ye s'pose them rigimints went to, when they got seperated so?"

"Why, one on 'em took the road to Trenton, ye know, to tell Cornwallis the news o' the mornin'. T'other helter-skeltered off cross-lots towards Brunswick, an' I guess there's where they've bro't up. They were completely routed, anyhow."

"I expected there'd be some sharp fighting, when we got to Princeton," said Zeb. "There was a rigimint there to protect the town, an' I s'posed they'd try to do it."

"Yes, an' 'twas wuth laffin' at to see how they did it. The idee o' them fine sojers leggin' it for college as soon 's they see us, an' shettin' themselves up in the big buildin's!"

"That was well enough," said Zeb, "if they'd only fit arter they got there; but you see, jist as we got some of our cannon fix'd for 'em, and let on some six pounders, they took it int' their heads that 'twas best to give up, or go to Brunswick."

"Ah, yes," said Zeke, "and we surrounded the college too quick for 'em. Thar' wasn't many on 'em got away to Brunswick. They say we got three hundred pris'ners."

"Have you heern what the loss is?"

"They say we lost nigh a hundred killed, but it's thought the inimy 've lost more. Howsumever, it's a *vict'ry*, anyhow."

Cornwallis never forgave himself for his blunder in not attacking Washington as soon as he arrived at Trenton. As his army was in all respects in better condition than the American's, he would probably have defeated them then. It is said that when the British reached Trenton, Sir William Erskine, one of the English officers, urged Cornwallis to attack the Americans immediately. Cornwallis thought there was no necessity for this. He said, " The rebels are so hemmed in by the Delaware, filled with ice, on one side, and Crosswick's Creek in their rear, that it is impossible for them to retreat, and I can make sure work of them in the morning."

To this Erskine replied:

"If Washington is the general I take him to be, his army will not be found on its present ground in the morning."

Erskine, as we have seen, was correct.

Cornwallis was disappointed and chagrined that the prey, which he thought was certainly his, had so completely escaped. But he was still more mortified when he learned of the victories they had achieved over the three regiments in his rear. Retracing his steps to Princeton, he entered one part of the town just as Washington left the opposite side, taking with him some three hundred prisoners.

As the object of Cornwallis was to proceed to Brunswick, to protect a large quantity of stores, ammunition and gold, which he had left there, he did not follow the army of Washington, who had taken a different road, but pressed rapidly on to Brunswick.

CHAPTER XVII.

RECAPTURE OF THE "GENERAL MONK."

On a summer day, early in this century of grace and liberty, two sociable old salts were sitting upon the fragment of a broken mast on one of the wharves at Baltimore. One of them was dressed in dark woolen trowsers, red shirt, a black neckerchief tied in a loose knot, and a low-crowned tarpaulin hat, garnished with a black ribbon an inch wide, with the two ends flapping over his ears like streamers. The other had on a pair of white duck pants, with short waist, large legs (one of which contained cloth enough to make a boy's whole suit), and a loose navy shirt, with a large white star in each corner of the collar. His pants were kept in place in the usual sailor-fashion, without suspenders, allowing the shirt to "bag" over the waistband; and on his head was a kind of striped, four-pointed Spanish cap, which fell over on one side, imparting to him a rather rakish look for so old a man. But the veteran marine had never been a pirate nor a slaver, only a privateers-man. He and his gray companion were talking over old times, and especially the days of '76, and the war of Independence.

"That affair of Barney's was rather a bold stroke," said he of the tarpaulin, turning over a new leaf of mental history.

"Aye, aye," replied the marine of the striped cap. "That was about the prettiest piece o' sea-boxin' that I ever had a fist in."

"What, was you in that engagement?" inquired the tarpaulin.

"I warn't nowhere else, an' I wouldn't ha' been if I could."

"Then you know all about it. Jest light out,

an' giv' me the reckonin's; for all I larnt o' the matter I picked up from the papers, an' blest if I know whe'er they told the truth or not."

A request for a sailor's yarn was always most acceptable to the old marine, for, like many others of his class, he was never more at home than when relating his adventures at sea, so he at once began.

"Lemme see — yes, 'twas on the eighth of April, 1782, that we commenced our cruise under Lieut. Joshua Barney. Our ship was the Hyder Ally, of sixteen guns. She was in fine order, for the State o' Pensylvany fitted her out 'xpressly for that service."

"What service was it?" asked the tarpaulin.

"Why, you know the British privateers had been committin' great depredations along our coast, and it was high time to stop 'em. So we were sent for that purpose — to capture the English privateers, and make reprisals on English merchantmen.

"Wall, we sailed down the bay to the capes,

an' there we tacked off an' on, with our eyes all round the compass, lookin' out for booty. We'd begun to think we was on a Flyin' Dutchman chase, when, one day, the lookout in the tops sung out:

"'A sail! a sail!'

"'Where away?' yelled the officer of the deck.

"'East by north,' was the answer.

"'Another!' cried the top.

"'Yes, a *third!*' says he, again.

"Bless ye, ye oughter seen how 'xcited that made us. Up comes Lieutenant Barney on deck with his spy-glass, and, after a sharp look at the strangers, he pronounced 'em to be a brig and two ships, all belongin' to the enemy. Every man was ordered to his post, and the decks were cleared for action. We didn't have to wait long, for the British opened fire upon us as soon as they got in range. It's likely they 'xpected to see our flag come down in two minnits, bein' as they was three to our one; but they didn't see no such thing. Barney wasn't the man to strike his flag till he knew the reason why. The brig reached us first, but Barney allowed her to pass us without givin' her a single ball. He didn't seem to think her worth noticing. Soon the two ships made up to us, till the one that led lay to within pistol-shot.

"Barney's plan was formed in a minnit. He meant to fight by strategy. So he said to the quarter-master at the helm, "When I give the order to *port the helm,* you mind and *put the helm hard a starboard.'* The object of that was to make the enemy think he was makin' a move that would surely expose him to their guns, that would throw 'em off a few minnits, till he got the Hyder Ally where he wanted her.

"So that was all settled, and when the enemy's ship had got within easy hearin' of us, Barney give orders to fire; and I'm thinkin' the broadside we sent into the Englishman at that order made ripping and splitting enough to let him know what sort o' stuff we was, the first time.

We weren't to be frightened by a few extra sheets o' canvas, and longer spars. The enemy now got ready to board us. Barney held his fire till they got alongside, and then sung out through his trumpet, so he could be heard above all the noise and confusion o' both vessels, '*Port the helm!*' Now the Englishman knew that order would swing us beautifully around, so as to give him the advantage of us. He made no effort, 'cordingly, to interfere with it. But you may guess how he stared when he saw us swing right round the other way! Before he could fairly make out what we was up to, we lay in fine position, and begun to give him a most terrible rakin'.

"Then, I tell ye, we had savage work. Broadside to broadside, we pummeled and pounded one another, till there warn't hardly a whole spot in either of us. But we could fire faster'n the Englishman, and we almost cut him to pieces. Splinters flew, spars fell, blood flowed, sails spilt to ribbons, and both vessels reeled and staggered as if a thunder-squall had crossed 'em. During all this time Lieut. Barney was on the quarter-deck, in full view of the enemy's marines, and a mark for every shooter. Barney never was one o' yer men that gunpower can turn white. No fear in him, whatever.

"Wall, sir, so quick was the work that in *twenty-six minnits no less than twenty broadsides had passed between us;* and by that time the enemy 'd had enough. His flag come down, and we took possession, with hurras that shook the sky and sea. The deck was slippery with blood, and covered with splinters, and the cockpit was filled with wounded marines."

"What did she prove to be?" asked old tarpaulin, who had listened with the greatest attention.

"She proved to be the Gin'ral Monk," replied the old privateers-man. "It was an American vessel, but had been captured from us by the British. They had re-fitted her, and christened her with a new name. She carried eighteen nine-pounders, and one hundred and thirty-six men, and was commanded by Capt. Rodgers. Her name, when she belonged to us, was the Gin'ral Washington. I am glad her name was changed, for I should have been sorry to fight agin a craft that bore the name o' Washington.

"The losses weren't so great as might ha' been expected, considerin' the number o' shot we fired. The Gin'ral Monk had only twenty killed, and thirty-three wounded, and that was jest five times as many killed, and three times as many wounded as we had."

"What do ye mean by that?" inquired tarpaulin.

"I jist mean what I say," replied the old privateers-man, at the same time doing a sum in multiplication to prove the truth of his assertion. "We had four killed, and five times four makes twenty. Our wounded numbered eleven, and three times eleven is thirty-three; so you see the inimy lost five times as many killed, and three times as many wounded as we."

The newspapers of the time, in their account of this ocean battle, described above by one of the heroes of the affair, said: "Considering the great disparity of force, together with the fierceness of the action, and the brilliancy of manœuvring, it is justly considered one of the proudest achievments on our naval record."

CHAPTER XVIII.

THE WYOMING MASSACRE.

Throughout the whole period of the Revolution, the difference of opinion as to the right or wrong of the war which divided the people into "Whigs" and "Tories" continued to exist, and develop every degree of hatred, treachery and active hostility. The great majority of the nation were united in the sentiment that resistance to British tyranny was right, and that the proper course to be purused under the circumstances was, to declare independence of England, and then fight it out. But, at the same time, many were totally opposed to all this. These took sides with the mother country, and gloried in the name of Tory. Not seldom this difference of feeling and thinking divided the same family. Brothers were arrayed against brothers, and children stood in the relation of deadly enemies.

In the settlement of Wyoming, which was located in one of the loveliest valleys of Pennsylvania, and where, hitherto, a thousand families had lived in peace, this division on the exciting topics of the day was productive of terribly disastrous results.

The British, knowing that a considerable portion of these colonists were in sympathy with England, seized every opportunity to provoke their active partisanship, and kindle the Tory sentiment to open mischief against the patriot cause. They strove hard to set neighbor against neighbor, friend against friend, and relative against relative. These efforts were fearfully successful. Many of the Tories were induced to unite in arms with the wild savages of the country, who were in the employ of the English, and engage in one of the most sanguinary and terrific massacres, of their own friends and relatives, of which history gives any account. The following letter, from a lady who was a spectator of the horrible tragedy, and one of the few who escaped the slaughter, gives a condensed, but vivid description of its bloody scenes.

"BEAR CREEK, *July 7th*, 1778.
"MY DEAR, DEAR SISTER:—

"I seem to have had a terrible dream — an awful nightmare. Oh! can it be true? *Our beautiful settlement is no more! Wyoming is destroyed!* But even that could be borne, were it not that the mutilated forms and the charred bones of *our friends* lie with the ashes of the dwellings.

"It will sicken your heart to hear it, as it does mine to tell it. [Here follows a list of many mutual acquaintances and kindred, murdered.] · · · · The good, the beautiful, and the brave, trembling age and helpless infancy, were slaughtered promiscuously together. I am hardly composed enough to give you a connected account of the events, but, as far as the particulars have been told me, and my own terribly fresh recollection can testify, they are as follows.

"You know that a large number of our neighbors were Tories. These turned their backs on the settlement, and went out in hatred, to ally themselves with the British and Indians. On the 3rd of July (four days ago), they returned with a large number of others, Englishmen, half-breeds and savages, in all more than fifteen hundred. Whom do you suppose they chose for their leader? It was no other than that cold-blooded, cruel, Tory refugee, Colonel John Butler. They were prowling round the settlements for some days, but pretended that they designed no injury. We did not believe them, and our patriots took every possible precaution to protect us. A battle was fought, but the enemies were too numerous, and the men fled for shelter into our little fort. Butler surrounded the fort, and ordered them to surrender. As the defences were very weak, and the garrison and supplies insufficient, it was mere madness to attempt any resistance. The surrender was made, and the deceived patriots yielded themselves, only to be doomed to death. Many of our men, however, had gone to Forty Fort, near Kingston, where myself, and many other women, as well as children, had fled. The enemy now presented themselves before this fort, and Butler demanded its surrender. His own cousin, Zeb Butler, had command of the fort. But that made no difference. He was just as willing to kill him as any one else.

When the summons came to surrender, Zeb at first refused. He proposed that they should hold a conference at the bridge, outside of the Forty. To this the treacherous old John consented; so, as soon as he was ready, Zeb marched out of the fort, with four hundred men, to hold a parley with the enemy.

"To his astonishment there was no enemy to be seen. Zeb, supposing that they had relinquished their design of attacking the fort, and fled before some unknown alarm, commenced a pursuit. This was a fatal mistake. After proceeding two or three miles, they overtook some straggling Indians. On these they fired, when, to their horror, they found themselves caught in an ambuscade. With demoniac shouts and yells, more than a thousand tories and savages sprang up and attacked them on every side. So amazed were our friends at this terrible surprise, that at first they could not fight. But the officers speedily rushed forward, encouraged the men, and restored order. They now began to return the enemy's fire. But as the Indians and Tories were concealed behind rocks and trees, it was almost impossible to hurt them. Yet from behind their protections these cowardly scoundrels poured an incessant fire, shooting down their victims by scores. The patriots fought bravely, and strove long to stem the tide of death. But it was no battle — it was only murder — and the slayers were all on one side.

At length, when the little band saw their enemies in their rear, cutting off all hope of retreat to the fort, they offered to surrender. The offer was rejected with shouts of derision. They then called for quarter. The prayer was answered with volleys of musketry, which silenced the voice of the petitioners forever. Some threw away their guns; others prostrated themselves among the slain, and feigned death; others rushed wildly from point to point, everywhere met by the frightful yells of the savages, and by the death-dealing tomahawk and musket. No quarter was given. The fiendish enemy would be satisfied with nothing less than the entire annihilation of their entrapped victims. Of the four hundred and seventeen who left the fort, only fifty-seven managed to escape, leaving three hundred and sixty weltering in their blood upon the field. Although this was dreadful, it was only the beginning of our miseries.

"After this slaughter, the murderers returned to the fort, and again demanded its surrender;

and, as an argument to enforce their demand, they sent into the fort *a hundred and ninety-six scalps*, taken from the heads of our friends who had just been slain. O Rachel! can you fancy anything so horrible? Even now I almost shriek as I think of the agony and cries of the women and children at that fearful sight. Those bleeding relics hinted too plainly what their own fate might be. Besides, they had every reason to believe that their husbands', and brothers', and fathers' scalps were among the number so brutally exposed, and that the dead bodies of these loved ones were lying unburied where they fell.

"Colonel Dennison, who now had command of the fort, refused to capitulate. The enemy then surrounded the fort, and poured into it a terrific canonade. When nearly all the men in the fort were either slain or wounded, Colonel Dennison went out with a flag of truce to inquire what terms would be granted the garrison if they surrendered. The answer of Butler was true to his savage nature, and contained only two words, 'The hatchet.' Although Butler thus threatened to slaughter the garrison when they surrendered, Dennison hoped that he might not be unnecessarily cruel. At any rate, as he could hold out no longer with any hope of success, he was obliged to yield. After Butler got possession of the fort, he selected a few prisoners to keep for some special purpose, and then drove the remainder, with the women and children, into the houses and barracks, and fastened them in. He then set fire to them, and burnt them all together! Will the dying screams of those helpless victims ever haunt the heart of that arch-murderer? Alas! I forget. Col. John Butler *has no heart.*

Fortunately for me, I had left the fort just after the detachment went out with Zeb Butler. I knew the house of Uncle Barlow would not be molested, strong Tory as he is, and though one could scarcely trust the nearest Tory friend in those terrible hours, I felt sure of Cousin Jane's affection. Uncle being away in the army, I might at least count upon Jane to protect or conceal me for a little while. I ran to the house, and threw myself upon her kindness. She received me tenderly and gladly, and told me to fear nothing. She gave me a little attic room, with one small window which looked toward the fort, and there she and I spent a great part of that dreadful day. But for that timely shelter, when Col. Butler returned I must have mingled my dying cries with those of the many whom the monster forced to so cruel an end.

"After this, the British and Indians had everything their own way. Tragedies that cry to heaven, and make humanity ashamed, were enacted on every side. Men, women and children were butchered and burned, as if such work were holiday play. The frenzied enemy, with the torch in one hand, and the sword in the other, ran like demons through the settlements, carrying conflagration and carnage wherever they went.

"Our neighbor, **Capt. Badlock**, was seized by

the monsters, and, instead of killing him outright, they subjected him to inconceivable tortures, because he was a patriot officer. They stuck lighted pitch-pine splinters into his flesh, all over his body, and then placed him in the midst of a fire of dry wood, and in that awful manner consumed him. Two other officers, Ranson and Durkee, were thrown into the same raging flames, and, to prevent them from rising, they were held down upon the burning brands with pitchforks! Even this was not the worst. But how can my hand write more?

"I *must* tell you of Partial Terry — what a brutal wretch he has come to be — Partial Terry, your former schoolmate. His father took sides with the colonies, but he went over to the British. Fired with unnatural hatred, he sent word to his father that he hoped to wash his hands in his heart's blood! On the day of the massacre, he went to his old home, and there gratified his infernal wish! He murdered his father, mother, brothers and sisters, stripped off their scalps; and then cut off his father's head!! Another monster slew his own mother, his father-in-law, his sisters, and their infant children, and thus exterminated his whole family!

"These are only a few out of many instances of terrible barbarity which were perpetrated on that fatal day. Even the beasts of the field did not escape. Some were shot down, whilst others had their tongues cut out, and were left to linger in this mutilated condition.

"Uncle's house was protected by the British flag; and, through the love and kindness of Cousin Jane, I was preserved. She told me, however, that I had better leave the house, and escape out of the valley; for when the Tories returned, if they found that I was in the house, they might be so heated with the fury of the time, as to injure me. So, after dark, I secretly left the house, and, falling in with some other women, who had managed to escape, we started for this place, where, after a tedious and painful journey, we finally arrived in safety. Such is war! Though, personally, I feel that I have great reason for gratitude to my Heavenly Father, for carrying me through such awful peril unhurt, my heart is heavy with grief for the many, many victims — and for my own and many ruined homes.

"Sadly, but always lovingly,
"Your Sister."

CHAPTER XIX.

YORKTOWN DAY.

"Well, Mr. Comparison, how is your wound this morning?" inquired an old New Jersey farmer, of one of the American soldiers honorably sent home with a bad hurt from the last patriot victory.

The person addressed had received the cognomen of "Mr. Comparison" from his habit of contantly using comparisons in his talk, piecing out almost every idea with another one that begun with the word "like." His comparisons were by no means always graceful or truthful, and sometimes they amounted to sheer contrast and turned his descriptions into absurdities. He was an amusing genius, and on account of his mirthfulness he was quite a favorite in camp.

"Wall, sir," quoth Mr. Comparison, "my wound is like a hungry fish, it carries an open mouth."

"It don't heal, eh?"

"Wall, if it does, it heals like our troubles with Great Britain, very slowly."

"How did you get it?"

"Git it? where I ought to, sir: at my post, sir, doin' my duty, sir."

"At Yorktown, I suppose?" said the farmer.

"Nowhere else, sir."

"It's a great honor to be wounded in that battle."

"That's true, sir, for if I'm not mistaken that victory has left the King's cause in this country like a snake with its back broken. I reckon the war will be healed up before my wound is."

"As you were there, give me a little sketch of the affair; I should be pleased to hear it."

"Wall, sir, arter the French jined us, and Gin'ral Washington had drawn his troops together, we commenced digging our first parallel on the seventh of October (1781). We commenced in the night, and worked as still as thunder, and by morning we had a trench dug nearly two miles long, besides erecting some redoubts. When the sun rose, the inimy found out we hadn't been dreaming through the night. Our long line of dirt showed what we'd been about, so they complimented us with a salute o' balls. They didn't do us any injury, though. Their cannon were only like great iron dogs that could bark loud enough but couldn't bite. The next night we erected some batteries in front of our parallel, and planted some cannon there with which to hold a conversation with the cannon of the inimy the next day. When these war ready, Gin'ral Washington came along and the cannon being loaded he touched off the first one himself. That was the signal for a tremenjus discharge — cannon and mortars roar'd all together. In a few nights more we had our second parallel-trench dug, and batteries planted much nearer to the English than afore. We kep' nearing 'em and nearing 'em jist like tide water on the flood."

"Didn't they fire on you?" inquired the farmer.

"Fire on us! why, sartin. Their balls and shell kep' comin' in all the time like hot punkins. There was two redoubts, or small forts, some three hundred yards in front o' their principal defences. These gin us consid'able trouble. So it was determined to take them at night with the baggernet. A brigade under La Fayette was assigned to the one on our right, and Col. Hamilton with another brigade was app'inted to take the one on our left. About eight o'clock at night the attack commenced. Our soldiers stepped up with their baggernets in rest, like schoolboys marchin' in to dinner — and, sir, they carried both o' them forts without firing a single shot. There was a bit of a tussel when the boys got in, and some was killed on both sides — but the job was done quick, sir, and done clean. Whilst this affair was going on, Gin'ral Washington with his staff was standing in a position open to the enemy's fire. Kurnel Cobb, one of his aids, said to him, 'Sir, you are to much exposed here; hadn't you better step back a little?'"

"Did he do it?" asked the farmer with no little curiosity.

"Do it?" echoed the wounded soldier. "No, but he jist answered by saying, 'Kurnel Cobb, if *you* are afraid, you have liberty to step back.' Cobb didn't advise the old Gin'ral any more, but they said he looked as awk'rd as a wheelbarrer, for a minute an' a haff.

"Wall, arter a few days all our parallels and batteries was done, and then we begun to s'lute the inimy, and send in our kairds. Pretty soon the bombs made 'em a visit, right where they lived, and tore away their defences, shattered their guns, blew up their houses, and finally old Conwallis had so many hot loaves in his oven that he was 'bleeged to cry enough,' and send over a flag of truce. That was on the eighteenth. On the nineteenth the old fellow surrended, and all his army. I ain't a goin' to brag, neighbor, but between you'n' I an' the liberty pole, that was a glorious day. My wound was swelled, and smarted like a rat-bite, and I had to keep in. But I holler'd hurra in the hosp'tal. There was one thing wantin', though, to the ceremony o' that s'rrender. When the inimy marched out o' their tents to give up their flags and themselves to the 'Mericans, Cornwallis warn't thar. He said he was sick, an' I guess he was. Sick or bashful — it don't make much odds which — Leastways he stayed in quarters like a turkle in his shell, and his officers had to bear the honors o' the day without him."

"I don't blame the man for not wantin' to

show himself, considerin' how little there was left of him."

"No, as the nigger said, 'Mass'r Washin'ton had shelled all de *corn* off'n him.' Cobwallis wouldn't a' looked well on parade anyhow."

"Ha, ha, and I reckon the old man knew it. Wall, I was down to camp that day, an' I got thar jist in time to see the ceremony."

"Good luck, you did! Now tell us how it struck ye. A good story's never spile't by being told twice, as the chaplain said about his old sermon."

"Wall, I come to town early in the mornin' with a load o' hay, and arter gittin' red o' that, I hung round till twelve o'clock. Then I heerd the drums beat, and in a few minutes the Americans and French troops come marchin' out o' camp. They took p'sition along the road and their line reached more'n a mile.

"The Americans were on the right side of the road, and the French were on the left. Gin'ral Washington was at the head of the American line, and Count Rochambeau on the opposite side o' the road was at the head o' the French. I was astonished at the great number o' spectators. The news must ha' spread like wild-fire to bring sich a multitude o' folks together. Every eye was bright and every face looked pleased. All the roads, except the one occupied by the soldiers, were filled with horses, chaises and carriages of all descriptions, loaded with spectators. About two o'clock the British army begun to file out with their music playin'. I tell ye, friends, they looked handsome, for Cornwallis had gin 'em a bran new suit o' uniform, and this was the first time they'd had it on."

"Didn't see *their colors*, did ye?" asked the wounded soldier.

"No," replied the farmer, "their flags were rolled up and tied, or cased, so that we didn't get a gimpse of the red cross nor the lion and the unicorn."

"Them beasts was caged that day," said the soldier.

"Yes," said the farmer, "it wasn't the lion chasin' the unicorn, but the Yankees leadin' the lion and the unicorn both all round the town."

"Ye minded how they carried their arms, didn't ye!" inquired the soldier.

"The officers had their side arms, and the men carried their muskets kinder lopped down, all jist alike. So they passed along the road between the French and American lines, lookin' sullen and mortified in the face. They was dressed a great deal better'n our army, but they didn't step smart, nor hardly reg'lar. Fact, some on 'em didn't hardly keep their ranks."

"Ye see they didn't care then whether school kep' or not," remarked Mr. Comparison. "One thing, neighbor, they say everybody was quiet an' still — didn't shout nor hurra there. Was that so?"

"That was so. Everybody seemed to kinder pity that whipped army, as if they was sorry enough a' ready, and 'twas too bad to crow over 'em. But you ought'n seen how the heads stretched up, and all eyes strained, to ketch a glimpse o' Cornwallis. One said, 'Where is he?' another said, 'That's him!' 'I see him, I see him!' said somebody else. 'La,' said an old woman near me, 'he's nothin' sich a lookin' cretur as I took him to be.' When the truth was known there was a great deal o' disap'intment all round. It's jist possible if Cornwallis *had* a showed himself, there might ha' been *some* shoutin' an' crowin'. The man that had druv our army 'afore him out and in 'twould a' been a treat to see on exhibition. Gin'ral O'Harra, who was appinted by Cornwallis to give up the sword, was s'posed by a good many to be Cornwallis himself, but they pretty soon found out this mistake. When O'Harra, with the conquered troops marchin' slowly behind him, reached the head o' the American line, he come up to where Gin'ral Washington and the other gin'rals was, and takin' off his cap he made an apology for the absence of his chief commander.

Washington, in a very polite manner, pointed him to Gin'ral Lincoln from whom he received instructions what course to pursue. Gin'ral Lincoln then conducted the army of pris'ners into a large field where I reckon the most painful duty of all was performed."

" You mean — " said the soldier.

" To give up their arms — " said the farmer.

" Ground arms," corrected the soldier.

" Yes, that's it. It wasn't done with a very good grace though. The officers gave the command to '*ground arms*' as though they were mad. and then many of the soldiers, instead of laying their muskets gently on the ground, dashed them on the pile violently as if they tried to break them. Some confusion was created, but Gin'ral Lincoln rode up to them and soon checked it."

" Ah, neighbor. it was a glorious day. and I don't wonder that when the messenger carried the news to Congress that Cornwallis was conquered, the door-keeper was so overjoyed that he fell dead. It isn't often that news is so good as to kill a body. It's like honey drowning a fly. Halloo, there's the surgeon. I must go now and have my wound dressed."

CHAPTER XX.

A GLIMPSE OF OLD '77.

HAVING occasion some months since to visit Albany, I was introduced to the B — family by whom I was treated with the greatest hospitality. Their ancestors were deeply interested in the American Revolution. Several of them were soldiers in the American army, and a grandfather was wounded at the battle of Saratoga. As might be expected, our conversation embraced repeated allusions to the events of the war, as Mrs. B — abounded in traditionary anecdotes which had been handed down in the family from those who had been actors in the scenes.

In one of our interviews, Mrs. B — incidentally remarked that there was an old revolutionary manuscript up in her garret which might be interesting to those who could read it, but for her own part, she found so much difficulty in deciphering it that it destroyed all her pleasure. She never made the attempt but once, and then gave up in despair. Professing to be something of an antiquarian, I asked permission to see the papers. She said they were in a barrel filled with old books, yellow newspapers and other cast-off materials, but she would ransack for them and upon my next visit I should see them.

Accordingly, when I called again, they were put in my possession. They were large sheets of foolscap paper, smoke-colored and stained with dirty water. They were written in a small hand, very angular, the letters not connected, and having somewhat the appearance of irregular *italics*. At first I found it exceedingly difficult to read a sentence, but after becoming accustomed to the letters, the writing became comparatively plain, and I could proceed with ease. The papers proved to be a journal of the war, kept by some patriot non-combatant, possibly a disabled officer of the American army. I take from it the following entries:

September 12*th*. 1777. I am now at Stillwater, in the state of New York. The American and British armies are approaching each other with a view, ultimately, to an engagement.

13*th*. I have just heard of the massacre of Miss Jenny McCrea, by some Indians in the employ of the British. She was engaged to be married to a refugee officer by the name of Jones. When the Americans left Fort Edward, she stayed behind, expecting to meet her lover, and by him to be led to the altar of Hymen. Instead of that, she was seized by two savages, who soon got quarrelling as to which of them should have the charge of her, when one of them became enraged, and to defeat the other, he suddenly struck her with his tomahawk and then scalped her. This piece of Indian tragedy has produced a profound sensation among the Americans.

14*th*. Burgoyne, the commander of the British, has employed the American savages to fight against us, and allows them to take scalps. This he has done, although he knows what terrible barbarities they practice in war, and upon their prisoners.

15*th*. Intelligence has reached us that Burgoyne has crossed the Hudson River and made a stand at Saratoga, a place where there are some remarkable mineral springs. General Gates is determined to face him, and if possible drive him into Canada.

16*th*. Gates has issued a proclamation to his troops to fire them with courage and revenge. Among other things he says: "If the murder of aged parents, with their innocent children; if mangling the blooming virgin and inoffensive youth are inducements to revenge — if the righteous cause of freedom, and the happiness of posterity, are motives to stimulate to conquer their mercenary and merciless foes, the time is now come, when they are called on by their country, by their general, and by every thing divine and human, to vanquish the foe."

17*th*. I am informed that our army is progressing towards the British in three columns, commanded by Generals Gates, Lincoln and Arnold. The officers and troops are in good spirits, and panting to meet the foe.

19*th*. We heard to-day loud firing in the direction of Bemis' Heights. A severe action must have occurred; we are all very anxious to learn the result.

20*th*. We have learned the particulars of the affair of yesterday. Gates and Burgoyne, with their respective armies, met and soon became engaged in a bloody contest. The Americans numbered twenty-five hundred. The whole army of Burgoyne was more than twice that number, though I have not learned how many of them were engaged. For three hours the firing on both sides was tremendous. Sometimes one regiment would be repulsed, but being reinforced would rally again, and drive their pursuers back. This was the case with both armies, so that their dead and wounded were mingled together. Some of our soldiers ascended high trees in the rear, and on the flanks of the enemy, and from their lofty points of observation they singled out the British officers and shot them. At one time Burgoyne, it was supposed, was aimed at and wounded, but it afterwards proved to be one of his aids who was delivering to him a message. The reason of the mistake arose from the fact that the saddle of the aid was ornamented with rich lace, from which it was inferred that he must be the commander.

After fighting with great fury until evening, the battle was suddenly terminated. In one part of the field the British retreated, and in another part the Americans gave way. Both parties claimed the victory, but the advantages were greatly in our favor. It is said that the enemy lost more than five hundred in killed, wounded and prisoners. On our side sixty-four were killed, two hundred and seventeen wounded and thirty-eight missing. After the firing had ceased, our army retired to their camp without being pursued, whilst the enemy lay all night upon their arms at a considerable distance from the field of action.

Oct. 2nd. Burgoyne is now in very trying circumstances. His retreat towards Canada will be very difficult and dangerous, and his advance to Albany on the Hudson is impossible. He has been expecting assistance from the troops at New York under Sir Henry Clinton, but is disappointed, as nothing is heard from Sir Henry. If this help arrives in time, it may be disastrous to the Americans.

Burgoyne's condition is constantly becoming worse on account of the numbers of Canadians and savages who are deserting him.

5th. I have been informed that the British commander has thrown up a long line of entrenchments in front of his camp, and is taking all other measures in his power to strengthen his position. He evidently expects another severe engagement in a short time. I intend, to-morrow, to go to the American camp, and, if possible, get an opportunity to witness an engagement.

3rd. Arrived in camp this afternoon and found our troops in good spirits and anxious to have another battle with the enemy.

8th. Yesterday the two armies met at Bemis' Heights, when a very bloody contest between them ensued. Colonel Morgan with his sharp-shooting rifle-men, sustained by Major Dearborn with a detachment of infantry, commenced the conflict with a furious attack upon the British grenadiers under the command of Major Ackland. In a short time the roar of battle was heard along the whole line of the two armies. Both parties fought with the greatest courage.

Death seemed robbed of his terrors. As fast as breaches were made in the ranks, the places of those who had fallen were supplied by others ready to expose themselves to a similar fate. The hated Hessians were on the right of the English. They fought at first with great valor, but were out-flanked by a detachment of our troops. Finally, after a severe conflict in which prodigies of valor were displayed in both sides, the whole British line, under the immediate command of Burgoyne himself, was broken and compelled to retreat in disorder. Then the Hessians, who until this time had remained firm, were assaulted with such intrepidity by Gov. Learned and Col. Brooks that the works, which had been erected for their protection, were gallantly taken; they were driven to their tents, and the whole of them, with all their equipage and stores, captured. Our troops gained a complete victory, and as might be expected, were intoxicated with joy. Colonel Cilley, who had acted nobly during the engagement, got astride of a brass cannon as though it were a war-horse, and there shouted and waved his cap with the greatest exultation. A number of valuable officers on both sides were either slain or wounded. General Frazer, a highly esteemed British officer, fell under the following circumstances. He was about changing the disposition of some of his troops, in order to go to the relief of others who were in danger of being overcome by the Americans. Col. Morgan saw him, and pointing him out to two or three of his best marksmen he said, "Do you see that gallant officer? that is General Frazer—I respect and honor him, but it is necessary he should die." That was enough. The riflemen immediately aimed; their weapons spoke, and Frazer instantly fell with a mortal wound and was carried to the rear. He was taken to the house of Baron Reidesel, where he was kindly nursed by the Baron's wife till he died. Night put an end to the engagement, or we might have taken the whole British army. We had between three hundred and four hundred killed and wounded, whilst the loss of the enemy approached six hundred.

CHAPTER XXI.

THE CAPTURE OF GENERAL BURGOYNE.

The following narrative is a continuation of the old journal found in the B—— family at Albany.

Oct. 9th, 1777. Those who have examined the field of battle say that they saw a hundred of the enemy lying dead and unburied upon the ground. We have learned that at the engagement on the 7th, Burgoyne came near losing his life. One bullet tore his waistcoat, and another passed through his hat. It was a narrow escape. These, however, are common in battle.

10th. Last night Burgoyne silently retreated.

He built numerous camp-fires, left a few tents standing so as to deceive us, and then, in the darkness, marched towards Saratoga, leaving three hundred sick and wounded, and two hundred barrels of flour, behind him. General Gates intends to cut off his further retreat. I hope he will be successful.

13*th*. Burgoyne, in his retreat, has been guilty of destroying all the property in his power. He has burnt every house that he could reach. The splendid mansion of General Schuyler he has levelled to the ground. He is evidently greatly chafed in consequence of his embarrassed circumstances. These are becoming worse, daily. General Gates has disposed of his troops in such a manner that they nearly surround the British army. If another battle occurs, the English are in a condition to be entirely cut to pieces. We have been fearful that Sir Henry Clinton may send some encouraging message to Burgoyne, or perhaps offers of assistance. But these fears were dispersed by the following singular incident. After the capture of Fort Montgomery, Sir Henry Clinton dispatched a messenger with the news to Burgoyne. This man was Daniel Taylor. On his way to Burgoyne's camp he was seized by our soldiers as a spy. He was seen to put something in his mouth and swallow it. This fact was communicated to the American general, George Clinton, who immediately prescribed for him a strong emetic. This produced the desired result. It made him throw up from his stomach a small silver bullet. This bullet was hollow, and made in two pieces, which were fastened together by a screw, on the rim, or edge. Being unscrewed, it was found to contain a letter from Sir Henry to Burgoyne, giving a brief statement of his success, but at the same time adding, " I cannot presume to order, or even advise, for obvious reasons." This showed that Sir Henry had no intention of " ordering " any portion of his troops to the relief of Burgoyne. This was great relief to us. This bullet was evidence that the prisoner who had swallowed it was a spy. He was tried, found guilty, and hung.

14*th*. To our unspeakable joy, General Burgoyne has to-day sent a flag of truce to our camp, with proposals to surrender. He asks a cessation of hostilities until the terms of capitulation can be agreed upon by the two parties. General Gates has complied with his request.

17*th*. It has been agreed between the two generals that the British army shall march out of their camp with the honors of war and their field artillery, to the place designated for that purpose, where their arms shall be piled at the command of their own officers. The troops are to be allowed to return to England, with the understanding that they are not to serve against us again during the war. The officers are to be treated according to their rank, and allowed to wear their side-arms. The Canadians are to be allowed to return home, on condition of their not fighting again against the United States.

This morning the American troops marched

into the British lines of defence to the soul-inspiring tune of Yankee Doodle. The royal army then marched out, and deposited their arms in the place appointed.

By this arrangement, General Gates spared his enemy the mortification of disarming themselves in the presence of their conquerors. This is regarded as characteristic of the amiable and benevolent disposition of Gates.

During the discussion of the terms of capitulation, two or three incidents occurred which came near defeating the surrender and opening the fighting anew.

In the first place, before the articles of agreement were signed, several hundred of the New York militia, whose term of enlistment had expired, marched away from camp without the permission of General Gates. About the same time, Burgoyne received information through a spy, that Sir Henry Clinton had taken Fort Montgomery, and would endeavor to force his way to Albany. When Burgoyne heard of both these events, he desired to recede from his proposal to capitulate. Though the articles of agreement were all arranged, adopted and signed by the officers who had been appointed for that purpose, and were merely wanting the signature of Burgoyne himself; yet, instead of signing them, he sent a note to General Gates, stating that he should recede from the treaty, because a part of the American troops had been detached from the army during the negotiation, and, with cool effrontery, if not with impudence, he required permission to send two officers to our camp to ascertain the fact. To this, of course. Gates would not consent. Being indignant at such conduct, he sent Lieutenant-Colonel Wilkinson to see Burgoyne personally, and say to him that if the treaty was not immediately ratified, hostilities would recommence. After a good deal of hesitation on the part of Burgoyne and his officers, he finally signed the document.

By this victory we have obtained possession of five thousand and eight hundred officers and soldiers, among whom are six members of the British parliament, forty-two brass cannon, seven thousand muskets, seventy-two thousand cartridges, and a great quantity of shot, shells and other munitions of war; with tents and clothing for seven thousand men.

Among the prisoners were two thousand and four hundred Hessians, whom the British had hired to fight against us.

The most important ceremony of the surrender was performed by the two commanders, — that was the delivering of the sword of the conquered into the hand of the victor in token of his submission. This simple but significant service was as follows: the two armies were drawn up in military order, in such a manner that they might both witness the ceremony. General Burgoyne, and General Gates, his conqueror, came out of the marquee of the latter together. They walked a short distance in front, in silence. Presently Burgoyne took a step back, drew his sword and handed it to the

American general. Gates received it with a gentlemanly bow, and then gracefully returned it to his vanquished opponent. After which, they returned again to the marquee. All this was done in silence; but, though there were no addresses, the occasion produced a profound impression.

Burgoyne had come to this country with the command of an army of some ten thousand men, provided abundantly with all the munitions of war. He declared that his army was never to retreat. He circulated through the colonies a variety of high-sounding, bombastic proclamations, sometimes filled with threatenings of bloodshed and conflagration, and at other times calling upon the people to send their deputies to him, supplicating his pardon and protection. Yet here he is, with his army conquered, himself a prisoner, and all his proud boasting proved to be vanity.

This victory will greatly dispirit the royalists in all parts of the country, and at the same time will fill the hearts of the friends of liberty with encouragement and joy.

I must not forget to mention that General Gates was greatly dependent upon the heroic efforts of General Arnold, and the skill and bravery of Col. Morgan's riflemen, for the successful issue of the conflict.

I intend to-morrow to ——

Here the journal ended. The remainder, if there had ever been any, was torn off and lost.

CHAPTER XXII.

THE BRAVE BRITISH WIFE.

On the ninth of October, 1777, Lady Ackland, the wife of that gallant British officer, Major Ackland, who had followed her husband to the war, received the painful intelligence that her husband had been shot in the Battle of Stillwater, and was a prisoner in the hands of the enemy. The information was astounding, and overwhelmed her with grief. The Baroness Reidesel, who was with her, endeavored to comfort her by telling her that his wound was only slight, and she had better get a permit to go over to the American camp and take care of him. She resolved so to do. Her application to the British General for permission to pass into the American lines resulted in her obtaining a letter from Burgoyne to General Gates, informing him of her object and asking his protection. The night was dark. The rain poured down. The air was cold. If she started she must go by water in an open boat, and incur the risk of being fired at by sentinals before she could explain to them her name and errand. But her anxiety was so great to reach her husband and know the worst of his condition, that she allowed none nor all of these considerations to daunt her. Obtaining a boat, and taking with her a few attendants, off she started in the darkness and storm to find her wounded husband. She arrived at the American out-posts, chilled with the cold, and drenched with the rain. Instead of allowing her to pass, the sentinal detained her till Major Dearborn, who was the officer of the guard, could be sent for. Upon his arrival he gave her permission to land; escorted her and her companions to the guard house; refreshed her with a cup of tea, and furnished her with the best accommodations in his power. In the morning, General Gates was informed of her condition. Deeply sympathizing with her in her affliction, he provided an escort for her protection; treated her with all the kindness of a parent, and gave orders that she should be treated with the consideration due to her sex, rank, character, and circumstances. She was soon after conveyed to Albany, where she had the unspeakable satisfaction of finding her husband and ministering to his wants.

To appreciate the bravery and fortitude of this adventure, it must be remembered that Lady Ackland had not been brought up to hardships. "She was a woman of the most tender and delicate frame; of the gentlest manners; habituated to all the soft elegancies and refined enjoyments that attend high birth and fortune. · · · Her mind alone was formed for such trials."

CHAPTER XXIII.

THE BATTLE OF BENNINGTON.

General Burgoyne's army had left Canada with the view of reducing, once for all, the obstinate Yankee Colonies into subjection to Great Britain. They had captured Fort Edward and were marching on, flushed with high hopes, when they were unexpectedly and completely stopped at Bennington. Burgoyne knew that at this place large numbers of cattle were collected for the use of the American soldiers. There also were large quantities of corn, flour, and other articles necessary for an army, deposited. He therefore sent a detachment of five hundred men, some of whom were cavalry, and one hundred Indians, all under Colonel Baum, to take Bennington by surprise and get possession of the cattle and stores there. The result of the attempt will be learned from the following conversation of two petty officers, which occurred the next morning.

"Hallo, Corporal, yesterday's affair was a pretty good programme, pretty well filled."

"That's true, Serjeant. Shake hands on it. Show me the Yankee that isn't happy to-day!"

"Good reason. Our victory was something to boast of, and the Tories can't say *this* time it was more by hit than wit."

' Colonel Baum had a capital position on these heights. And his redoubts here are no mean affair for a first-class soldier."

"Ah," replied the Corporal, "and he defended them well too. His Germans fought us like tigers for two hours. But they couldn't stand our old fire-locks. How they did hate to run, though, when we rushed them out of their entrenchments, and across the brook yonder!"

"I tell you, Baum was an old war-horse. But he found his match when he met Jno. Stark."

"Did you ever see anything finer than Stark's disposition of our troops?"

"I don't know what the disposition of the troops was. I only know that all hands fought splendidly on both sides — except those sneaking Indians who filed off between the armies, early in the battle, and dodged out of harm's way."

"Well, the plan was this: Colonel Nichols was sent with two hundred men to attack the rear of the enemy's left; and Colonel Herrick with three hundred was commanded to fall upon the rear of the enemy's right. There, you see, was a master-stroke to begin with. *Then* Colonels Hubbard and Stickney were ordered to advance with two hundred men on the right, and one hundred men in front, whilst Stark himself came up slowly and supported the hundred with all his reserve."

"Why, that was spreading a complete net for them," replied the Corporal.

"See now how it worked. At three o'clock yesterday afternoon, Colonel Nichols opened his fire upon the rear of the enemy's left. Then Herrick's men attacked the rear of the enemy's right; all according to arrangement. Well, while these were galling them so from behind, Hubbard and Stickney's men were performing their assigned parts in the play, and Stark coming up in front with his troops, there was no way for the enemy, you see, but to fight it out in a general engagement, and win or lose at one throw. They held their ground bravely, but Stark had put the whole strain on them at once, and when they broke and retreated at five o'clock it was almost a matter of course. I think there was as much skill in the plan, as valor in the fight — and one deserves as much credit as the other for the victory."

"And yet," said the Corporal, "we came near losing the day after that."

"So we did," added the Sergeant, "and had not a kind Providence favored us, we should be retreating now. The trouble was, as we had driven off the German and British troops, and the day seemed to be certainly ours, the militia left their colors and scattered off the battle-ground for plunder. They expected that many of the enemy who had fallen had money, watches, or other valuable articles in their possession, and they were resolved to obtain them. It was while they were off engaged in this treasure-hunting, that Colonel Brehman, with his five hundred Grenadiers, light infantry and chasseurs, came unexpectedly to the relief of the British, I half believed our fortune had turned when he rallied the beaten army and drove us back. But the tide didn't set that way long. Up comes Colonel Warren's regiment of Continentals jist in time. He throws his whole weight on Brehman. The scattered militia get into battle-line; we fight the ground over again; and away goes

Brehman leaving his artillery and baggage behind him."

"Don't you fancy, Sergeant, that the result might have been different if Baum hadn't been mortally wounded?"

"Hardly. But he was a brave and able officer, and one whom even Stark might feel proud to conquer."

CHAPTER XXIV.

WASHINGTON'S FAREWELL.

By the unanimous vote of Congress, Washington was chosen Commander-in-chief of the American army, and on the 2d day of July, 1775, in Cambridge, Massachusetts, he publicly entered upon the discharge of this important and responsible duty. The tree is yet standing, under which, on that impressive occasion, the officers of the army were gathered together, to welcome their new chief, and first recognize the wise leadership which made American Independence sure.

After that glorious result had been achieved, and there was no further occasion for the continuance of an army, Washington took leave of his officers, and returned, clothed with honor, to his quiet retreat at Mount Vernon. This parting of Washington from the brave officers of his army, with whom he had suffered hardship, and shared the perils of many battle fields, presented a scene of peculiar tenderness and solemnity. It occurred at Frances' Tavern, in the city of New York, on the 4th day of December, 1783.

About noon the officers of the army were assembled in one of the rooms of the hotel, and, whilst indulging in conversation with each other, the door opened and Washington entered. The feelings of his heart were too strong to be concealed. They betrayed themselves in his saddened countenance, and eyes that swam with tears. According to the custom of the times, he poured out a glass of wine, and raising it, said:

"With a heart full of love and gratitude, I now take leave of you; I most devoutly wish that your latter days may be as prosperous and happy as your former ones have been glorious and honorable."

He then raised the glass and drank. After which he said:

"I cannot come to each of you to take my leave, but shall be obliged if each of you will come and take me by the hand."

As General Knox was the nearest to him, he turned and extended to him his hand. Washington was unable to speak. He grasped the hand of his companion-in-arms, and then silently embraced him. It was a deeply touching scene. The other officers then followed, of whom he took leave in the same affectionate manner. There were no congratulations at the success of the war — no expressions of commendation — no "good-byes" and "God bless you." Not a word was uttered, though all eyes were filled with tears, and every heart throbbed with deep emotion. Dignity, silence and solemnity prevailed.

This being over, Washington left the room;

passed through a corps of light infantry, and proceeded on foot to the Battery, at the southern extremity of the city. He was followed by all the officers, soldiers, and a large crowd of spectators. Having reached White Hall, he entered a barge, turned to the assembled multitude, and raising his hat, he gracefully waved it, and bade them a silent adieu. The officers did the same; and after waiting until the barge, with its precious freight, had proceeded a considerable distance from the shore, they returned to the tavern.

Washington was taken by the barge to Paulus Hook. From there he proceeded slowly to Annapolis, in Maryland, where Congress was then in session, having adjourned thither from Princeton. Everywhere on the route he was received with testimonials of the highest respect and honor. There were processions, military displays, dinners, addresses, and public receptions, by legislatures of States, corporations of towns, scientific associations, and religious societies.

It was like a continual triumphant march. Throughout his whole course he was welcomed by the spontaneous sentiment of the people as the "Saviour of his country." No other military chieftain ever received such pure and strong manifestations of the esteem and love of a free people; no other was so deserving.

After reaching Annapolis, he informed the President of his readiness to relinquish the commission which he had received from Congress as Commander-in-chief of the American forces.

Accordingly, on the twenty-third of December, in the presence of all the members of Congress, and a large assembly of spectators, he publicly resigned his office. In so doing he delivered a calm, dignified and appropriate address, which he closed as follows:

"Having now finished the work assigned me, I retire from the great theatre of action, and bidding an affectionate farewell to this august body, under whose orders I have so long acted, I here offer my commission, and take my leave of all the employments of public life." He then stepped to the desk of the President of the Congress, and delivered into his hands his commission. The President, in receiving it, delivered an address in reply. Washington then left for Mount Vernon, and arrived there the same day, after an unbroken absence of eight years.

CHAPTER XXV.

COL. BRATTON'S WIFE.

"Some of the most gallant actions of the Revolutionary war were performed in the South." said a young man to one of the discharged officers of the Revolution, "and I hope whoever attempts to write its history will not fail to give an account of Huck's defeat."

"I have heard that it was a splendid affair, but I never learned the particulars," replied the officer.

"Well, sir, I will relate them as I heard them from one who was present in the action."

"I should be pleased to listen, as nothing gratifies me more than the narratives of those adventures. I was at the North at that time, or I should have learned the whole affair."

"Colonel Bratton," commenced the young man, "was a bold and skillful officer. None knew better than he how to watch and surprise an enemy, and often he would fall fiercely upon the British at unexpected hours, and spread havoc and destruction through their ranks. He became so troublesome to them that they determined to destroy him. That however was easier to propose than to do. Still, they made the attempt. They appointed Captain Huck, with four hundred men to pursue him, and hunt him down. Huck knew Bratton's residence (in Bratton'sville, South Carolina). So he came to the house one evening with a squad of men, and ushered himself without ceremony into the presence of the Colonel's wife.

"' Where's your rebel husband?' he inquired in a rough tone of authority.

"Without being moved she simply yet proudly replied, 'Where such good men as Col. Bratton ought to be; in Sumter's army.' Now Sumter was a real plague to the British, as they confessed; and hence the reply of Mrs. Bratton greatly incensed Huck. He however smothered his anger and said.

"'Your cause, Mrs. Bratton is in a bad condition. Your friends are coming over to our side, the side of his Majesty, and your soldiers can hold out but a short time longer, you had better inform me of Bratton's place of retreat.'

"'He has no place of *retreat* sir. Go to General Sumter if you want to know where my husband is posted.'

"'I tell you again, the rebel cause is desperate, Mrs. Bratton. It's a pity your husband should continue a whig when the tory side is destined to triumph. If you will prevail on him to unite with his Majesty's forces, he shall receive a commission in the army.'

"'I had rather see my husband perish a rebel, as you please to call him, than to see him wear the highest honors in the power of the king's officers to bestow.' This fearless reply filled the hearers with such indignation that one of the soldiers seized a reaping-hook that was in the room, and made an effort to cut her throat with it."

"Just like the murderous crew!" cried the officer, excited by the narrative of his young friend. "Just like them! They could cut down females and children without the least compunction."

"In this instance however the attempt was thwarted," said the young man.

"Glad of that," was the response. "How was it done?"

"Why, the officer who was second in command sprang forward; seized the would be murderer, and forcibly rescued the lady from her peril. Had it not been for his interference she would have been slain upon the spot. This humane deliverance on the part of the officer did not go unrewarded."

"What! did she pay him for doing no more than was his duty?"

"Not exactly; yet he did get his pay, as you will see before I get through."

"Well, the red-coats were not ready yet to leave the house. They were hungry, and the least they could do now by way of annoying Mrs. Bratton was to oblige her to get supper for them. After this they went to another house not far off and quartered there for the night, while his soldiers encamped near by. Of course, they intended next morning to resume their hunt for Col. Bratton.

"Now it so happened that Bratton himself had received information of their movements, and found where they were spending the night. With characteristic energy, he resolved at once to give them an unexpected visit, and if possible cut them off with a stroke. It was a daring, almost a reckless undertaking, for he had only fifty men, while Huck, as I have said had four hundred. Not knowing that their pursued enemy was so near, or that any enemy was at hand, Huck's men did not keep a vigilant guard. Their sentinels, if any were appointed, fell asleep at their post. The first they knew of any danger, they learned from the shouting and firing of Bratton's troops in the midst of them. As usual he had come silently and stealthily, upon them, and finding them asleep, had pounced upon them 'like a wolf on the fold.' Those who were not killed while dreaming, awoke, sprang to their feet, seized their weapons in confusion and dismay, and made a wild attempt to fight for their lives. It was all in vain, Bratton's men were cool, and knew their ground. Besides, they had all the advantage of the first move in the game. Consternation seized the camp, and though many resisted desperately their struggles effected little. Huck himself was slain, and then the command devolved upon the second officer, who had saved the life of Mrs. Bratton the evening before. He strove with great valor to rally his men, and stimulate them to make a vigorous defense. But a panic had seized them and they were beyond his control. As the men fled they were pursued. Thus the scene of action changed ground, and reached the premises around Bratton's house. The enemy were totally routed. Many were slain, and a number were taken prisoners, among whom was the second officer. As the British had treated with great inhumanity the Americans whom they had taken prisoners, putting many of them cruelly to death, the conquerers on this occasion determined to retaliate. Naturally the commander was first doomed. Some were opposed to his death, and remonstrated. Blood enough had been shed in the conflict they said. How could unnecessary cruelty on the part of the British, justify unnecessary cruelty in Americans? An example of *humanity* (they argued) would have a better effect upon the enemy than this useless shedding of a prisoner's blood. They were over-ruled however by the voice of the majority, and the officer was condemned to die.

When he was informed of his doom, he exhibited no unmanly fear; he asked no mercy. He simply requested to see Mrs. Bratton before he died. His request was granted. As soon as the lady saw him, she recognised him as the person who had saved her life when the enraged soldier brandished the reaping-hook at her throat. Influenced by gratitude she resolved to save her deliverer if it were in her power. She pleaded for him, and though at first his captors gave no heed to her entreaties, when she told them in glowing terms of the good deed by which the man had earned a better fate, their resolution began to waver.

"'But for his kind and timely interference I should not have been here alive. If you respect me, then for my sake spare him. You will not put my deliverer to death.' Her plea was successful. It is needless to say that with Col. Bratton, at least, such argument was omnipotent. The sentence was revoked, and the British officer was saved. 'Blessed are the merciful, for they shall obtain mercy.' That lady's kindness was none the less noble for illustrating one of the beatitudes so well."

"She was just the right kind of a woman for an officer's wife."

"That she was," replied the young man.

"There is another fact in her history that would prove it if any more proof was needed. She was as thoughtful and discreet as she was brave and kind."

"Let's have the fact," said the officer, impatient to hear more of this heroine of the South.

"At one time Colonel Bratton had stored, with great secrecy (as he thought), a large quantity of ammunition a short distance from his house. In some way, but how I never learned, the British obtained a knowledge of this, and resolved to seize the stores. A party of troops was dispatched for this purpose. Mrs Bratton heard of their advance and knew their errand. As it was impossible to remove the ammunition, she determined that, at least, the British should not use it. It would be less of a loss to the Americans to burn it all at once than to leave it to be made into cartridges for their enemies' guns. She therefore resolved to set it on fire herself. No time was to be lost.

"The British were coming and would soon be there. She prepared a slow match, or some sort of train, and laying it with care to the magazine awaited the approach of the enemy. As soon as she saw the plumes of the coming column, she touched the train, and fled to a safe distance. The fire slowly crept towards the powder. The British came rapidly along the road; but before they reached the house a loud explosion shook the ground and filled the air with smoke and flying fragments. Cheated thus out of their coveted booty, at the moment they were about to seize it, the wrathful and disgusted red-coats wheeled about, and marched back to their camp."

"Good, good!" shouted the officer in great glee, after hearing the young man's recital, "Good!" continued he, clapping his hands. "The brave woman! She ought to have a medal and a monument!"

CHAPTER XXVI.

THE CONCEALED GUARD.

ON the 23d of September, 1780, three plain, honest countrymen were concealed behind some bushes on the side of the road, on the eastern bank of the Hudson river, about half a mile above Tarrytown. At that time the British had possession of the city and surrounding suburbs of New York, whilst the Americans were encamped further to the North, their lines extending to White Plains. The country between the lines of the two parties was greatly exposed to incursions from the British, who would come up from New York, seize all the horses, cattle, grain and hogs they could find, and escape with them to New York. Voluntary patrol guards were established among the Americans who resided on this "neutral ground," to watch for these lawless incursions, and, by alarming the people, rouse them to resist and defeat the object of these military robbers. Another practice which such guards were intended to prevent was, the trading away of cattle, or property of any kind, by sly Tories, to the British below. Where this was attempted, the persons who succeeded in detecting the guilty parties were, by the law of the State, entitled to all the cattle or goods which they thus captured on their way to the enemy. It was customary, also, for the captors to take for their own use all the personal effects, as jewelry, money, etc., which they found upon their prisoners.

These were among the reasons which might have induced these three men to be lying here in ambush, for the purpose of seizing suspicious passers-by. The names of these three men were John Paulding, Isaac Van Wart and David Williams. They had lain some time in their concealment, when a man was seen on the crest of the hill, coming down into the valley.

"Some one heaves in sight," said Paulding.

"What is he?" inquired Williams.

The three men peeped through the bushes as well as they were able, until the traveler had nearly descended the hill, when Paulding said:

"He's no game for us. It's Neighbor Jones."

They did not accost him, nor reveal the place of their concealment. Two or three others passed by, whom they knew to be friendly to the American cause, and whom they did not interrupt.

There they remained till about ten o'clock, when a person on horseback made his appearance.

"Heigho!" said one of the party, "there comes a stranger."

"Yes," replied one of the others, in a low tone of voice, "he looks like a gentleman. He's well dressed, and has boots on; if you don't

Capture of Major Andre. Page 264.

know him you had better step out and stop him."

Upon that, Paulding arose from the ground on which he was sitting, stepped out into the road, presented his firelock to the breast of the stranger, ordered him to stand, and said:

"Which way are you going?"

Paulding had previously been taken a prisoner by the British. A good suit of clothes which he then had on were taken from him by the officer who had been in charge, and an old, worn-out British suit given him in their stead. A portion of this suit he now wore, and André, seeing the military buttons of this suit, naturally supposed that he was a Tory, or that he belonged to the British army. Hence he incautiously replied to Paulding's question by saying:

"Gentlemen, I hope you belong to our party."

"What party?" replied Paulding.

"The lower party," he answered.

The British were called the lower party, because they were garrisoned in New York, which was *down* the river, so that the stranger, by this reply, acknowledged himself to be an Englishman. In order to draw out of him all they could, the men who had stopped him pretended that they belonged to that party also. This threw the traveler entirely off his guard, and he at once said:

"I am a British officer, on particular business, and I hope you will not detain me a minute."

To convince them that he was a British officer, he showed them his watch. This was enough to satisfy the men that he was some important personage, and ought to be carefully searched.

Paulding therefore told him to dismount. The stranger was surprised, and suspected that his captors, instead of being, as they professed to be, on the side of the British, were in sympathy with the Americans; and that, consequently, he was a prisoner. Realizing that he had exposed his real character by acknowledging that he was a British officer, he exclaimed:

"My God! I must do anything to get along."

He then pretended that his statement of being on the side of the English was a mere hoax. That he was only jesting. Instead of being a British officer, he was an American.

"I am an American. My name is John Anderson."

"Where are you going?"

"I am going to Dobb's Ferry, to meet a person there who has got some intelligence for General Arnold."

He then took from his pocket General Arnold's pass, and showed it to them. It was as follows:

HEAD QUARTERS, ROBINSON'S HOUSE,
Sept. 22d, 1780.

Permit Mr. John Anderson to pass the Guards to the White Plains, or below if he Chooses, he being on Public Business by my Direction.

B. ARNOLD, *M. Gen'l.*

Paulding read this, and would have released

the prisoner if he had not previously said he was a British officer.

"I hope," said Paulding, "you will not be offended, sir. We do not intend to rob you. There are many bad people on the road, and we did not know but you might be one. Please step this way, sir."

The stranger having dismounted, they took him one side, and told him to undress. As he took off his clothes, they examined every pocket, felt between the linings, and made a thorough search, but could find nothing. They looked into his hat. There was nothing there. They then told him to take off his boots. Without the least reluctance he complied. After pulling off one of his boots, the men looked in and felt in, but there was nothing there. They then felt the bottom of his foot, and found there was something between the sole of his foot and the stocking.

"Please pull off your stocking, sir."

He did so, and in the bottom of it were found

three papers. Paulding opened them, and, after reading a portion of them, said:

"He's a spy!"

"Take off your other stocking, sir."

This also was examined, and three more papers were found. After having made this important discovery, the men told him to dress himself.

"What will you give us to let you go?" asked Paulding.

"I will give you any sum of money you'll name," he replied.

"Will you give us your horse, saddle, bridle, watch, and one hundred guineas?"

"Yes. And I will have them delivered at any point,—yes, even in this very spot, so that you may be sure to get them."

"Won't you give us any more?"

"Yes, I will give you any quantity of dry goods, or any amount of money, and send it to any place you will name."

"No," said Paulding, "if you would give us

ten thousand guineas you should not stir one step."

"Wouldn't you get away if you could?"

"Certainly I would."

"I don't intend that you shall."

The three men led their prisoner along, asking him questions on the way, until he requested them to ask no more, as he would reveal all when they brought him to some military commander. The nearest military post was North Castle, under the command of Lieut. Col. Jameson. Within a few hours he was taken thither, and delivered into the hands of Jameson, with all the papers that had been found in his stockings. Great was the surprise of his captors, when their prisoner confessed himself to be Major John André, Adjutant-General in the British army.

The papers which were found upon him proved to be very important documents. They contained a variety of valuable information, respecting the condition and resources of West

Point; how the army there were to conduct themselves in case they should be attacked, what were the weak points of their defences, and hints respecting the operations of the Americans in the approaching campaign. All of these papers were in the undisguised hand of Benedict Arnold. It was plainly evident that Arnold was a traitor, and André was a spy! When Arnold, who had command of the important post at West Point, and had furnished these dangerous papers to the enemy, learned of their capture, he immediately fled from the American camp, engaged six men to row him down the river, under a flag of truce, to the British ship Vulture, and then had the meanness to keep all the men prisoners on board the Vulture, and have them carried to New York. As soon, however, as they arrived there, Sir Henry Clinton, the British general, despising such contemptible conduct, set them all at liberty.

André was tried as a spy, found guilty, and hung. It was a subject of general regret that

Arnold could not have been substituted in his place.

According to the custom which, as we have said, prevailed, André's captors obtained his horse, saddle, bridle and watch. These were sold, and the money divided between the three men and four others who were in their company, and were watching on the top of the hill when André was taken.

CHAPTER XXVII.

DEBORAH SAMSON, THE GIRL SOLDIER.

It was a beautiful day in the summer of 1799, when an old lady and two young girls, who had been wandering among the moss-covered and almost obliterated grave-stones of the ancient cemetery on the hill of Plymouth, had seated themselves upon a low monument. This monument had the appearance of a sailor's chest, except that it was all of stone. The sides and ends were of red sand-stone, the top was a thick slab of blue slate-stone, with a death's head and cross-bones carved upon it, under which were inscriptions to the memory of those whose mortal remains were reposing beneath. The ancient gambrel-roofed houses of the early settlers, mingling with those of more modern date, extended along down the street, whilst the blue water of the bay where the famous May Flower rode out the storms of the pilgrims' first winter was reflecting the blue sky in the distance.

Among these ancient graves the ladies had been conversing respecting the courage, the patience, the firmness and the piety of the women of Plymouth, the inscriptions on some of whose graves they had been reading.

"Did you say, Grandmother, that women took part in the war of the Revolution?" asked the youngest, a blue-eyed little lassie with numerous flaxen ringlets falling around her sweet face. Like many a Plymouth girl, this pretty girl had received the poetic name of Rose, after Rose Standish, of course.

"Yes, childie, they took part in more ways than one."

"You don't mean that any actually went to

the wars and fought?" continued the blue-eyed and bright-minded girl.

"I know of one who did; and she was born in this very town."

"Who was she, and do we know any of her descendants?" inquired the older sister who was a short, plump, brunette. Her interest in the conversation had been slight until now.

"Her name was Deborah Samson."

"Do tell us all about her," said Rose. "I know it must be interesting. We should like to hear it, shouldn't we, Rachel?" And she settled down nearer her grandmother, so glad of a "story."

Grandmother began: "Well, you see, Deborah belonged to a family who had to work for a living. Her edecation was poor; though, while she went to school, which was only for a short time, she showed she had a good mind and a strong memory. When the Revolution broke out, Deborah at once became greatly interested in it. Her thought, day and night, was to do something to help the American cause. I heard her say more'n once, 'I'm sorry, *sorry*, SORRY I ain't a man! If I was, I'd shoulder a firelock and march agin the Red-coats!'

"By industry and economy Debby had managed to lay up ten or twelve dollars. She finally determined to spend this vast sum in the cause of liberty. So she thought and thought how to do it; and the more she thought the more anxious she felt to do more than simply give this money to the " rebels," as the Americans were called.

"She was personally a brave girl, she had also a streak of romance in her nature, she had no strong family ties to prevent her from following out a fancy; and at last she made up her mind to enlist in the army herself, and, side by side with her countrymen, to fight agin the redcoats and drive them from the land —"

"*Would* they take a girl into the army, Grandma?" interrupted Rose.

"Not if they knew she was a girl. Debby

was aware of that. That was her great difficulty. But you know the old saying, 'Where there's a will there's a way.' Debby had the will to be a soldier, and Debby found a way. Mighty sly though she had to be," added the old lady with a shake of the head.

"I should think so!" said Rachel. "How *could* she do it? — do hurry, Grandmother!"

"Well, with her ten or twelve dollars, she bought a quantity of cheap fustian. Out of this she cut a suit of men's clothes. On these she worked whenever she could without being seen, or exciting inquiry. When she had finished one article, she carefully concealed it in a hay-stack a short distance from the house. She then worked upon another; and when that was completed she hid it in the same place. In this way the whole suit was made. This accomplished, she pretended she was dissatisfied with her wages where she was, and gave out that she was going to some other town in order to get more. So she tied up her new suit of fustian, and taking some few other articles, off she went. After getting out of town, she stepped out of the road into a retired spot. There, with a few good wholesome blushes, she threw off her woman's apparel, and put on the suit of fustian."

"I guess she looked pretty queer," said Rose, laughing.

"I guess she *felt* pretty queer?" said Rachel.

"I wonder if she knew herself when she looked into a brook, and saw somebody dressed in men's clothes looking up at her," said the pretty Rose, blushing into a very red Rose at the bare thought.

"Well, what did she do after she changed her dress?" inquired Rachel, returning to the story.

"She hastened to the American camp; and there, in October 1778, she enlisted in the army under the name of Robert Shirtliffe. She paraded with the men; she slept in tents; she stood sentinal; she performed all the duties of a common soldier."

"But did she fight?" inquired Rose.

"Fight? Certainly she did, childie! She was as courageous as any of the soldiers. In war, when any very dangerous enterprise is to be executed, and they want none but real brave men, they are accustomed to ask the soldiers to *offer* their services, that is, to go *of their own accord*. Those who will do so are called " volunteers;" and it is well known that none but the brave will volunteer. Well, I've heern it said that Debby was always one of the volunteers on such occasions, and that she would fight as courageously as the best on 'em!"

"I wonder she didn't get wounded sometimes."

"She *was* wounded two or three times, Rose. Once she was cut in the head with a sword. At another time she was shot through her shoulder. Her great fear was lest, being wounded, it should be discovered that she was a girl in disguise. She would rather have died in the battle.

"She was not discovered by her wounds; but

afterwards she was seized with brain fever. She suffered greatly. She feared that she would become delirious, and reveal her secret. In that case the shame of her exposure would be overwhelming. Her symptoms grew worse. Delirium did set in. She was taken to the hospital where were a large number of others, and, as a consequence, her case did not receive so much attention as it otherwise would.

"But one day, as the surgeon was taking his daily rounds, he inquired of the nurse, 'How is Robert?'

"The mournful answer was, 'Poor Bob is gone.' As the nurse saw no indication of life, she supposed that the patient was dead.

"The doctor approached the bed and examined the pulse. He found that it was feebly beating, he then attempted to lay his hand over the heart, and then — poor, brave, Debby! her secret was no longer her own! But the physician had both discretion and generosity. He paid her every attention, and when she had recovered sufficiently to be removed he took her to his own house. This step created considerable surprise in the doctor's family, but the young soldier soon became a favorite.

"Whilst she was in the doctor's house a very romantic incident occurred."

"Oh, what was that?" cried Rachel, eagerly.

"Well, the doctor had a niece, an' I heern tell she was a raal han'som body, rich, too. Well, this niece became very much interested in the sick soldier.

"They often, as the patient's health improved, took rides together; and finally the niece contrived to make known to the blushing Robert her attachment; and she contrived, too, to propose that they should get married."

"What a bold girl!" exclaimed Rachel.

"I think so myself," added the old lady, "and be sure it was a sore affliction to Debby. However, without pretending to return her attachment, she simply said they would 'see each other again.'

"After her full recovery, the doctor, with the permission of the captain of her company, gave her a letter to take to General Washington. Our quick-witted Debby immediately suspected she was discovered; and that this letter was intended to give the commander-in-chief a knowledge of her secret. However, as it was the duty of a soldier to obey orders, without asking questions, she carried the letter to head-quarters.

"When she went into the presence of Washington, all dressed in her regimentals, she was greatly agitated. The Gin'ral noticed it. He requested one of his attendants to take her out, and give her some refreshments.

"Whilst she was gone, Washington read the letter. When she returned, without saying a word, the Gin'ral put into her hand a discharge from the army. He also gave her a private note containing good advice, and a sum of money sufficient for her present wants. Debby often expressed her gratitude for the great kindness and delicacy with which Washington treated her — and, in fact, the good surgeon too."-

"Was she ever married, Grandma?"

"Yes, after the close of the war she married a Mr. Benjamin Gannett, of Sharon, Massachusetts.

"But come, dears, the sun is going down, and we must hurry if we would reach home before dark."

CHAPTER XXVIII.

SOLDIERS' YARNS.

AFTER the war of the Revolution was over, naturally enough the "old soldiers" who had been discharged from the army, dearly loved to tell over the incidents of their hard service, and amuse their friends with stories of both the written and unwritten events of their long campaigns. These stories were always listened to with keen interest by attentive hearers, gathered in stores and taverns, or around patriotic firesides.

Let the reader fancy himself one of a small but miscellaneous audience, in a certain New York inn, on an evening late in the autumn of the year 1800. Five veterans, representing as many regiments, and almost every section of Revolutionary service, were sitting there, hale old fellows well met, joking each other, and comparing ages, good looks, and personal exploits.

They had just eaten and drank together, and their tongues, loosened by good cheer, ran glib with the old jargon of the camp, and delivered curious and entertaining snatches of warlike history.

One of them, a big, loose-jointed Yankee, with high cheek-bones, and twinkling grey eyes, who was addressed as " Leftenant Longshort," because his clothes were always too scant for his size, had been toasting some of the favorite heroes of the old army, and when he came out with " Gin'ral Lincoln — a Solon in council, a Cæsar in war," a comrade took up the sentiment, and made it the cue for a little talk of his own. This man had served under Lincoln, and been severely hurt, so that he was much grown out of shape ; but he made light of his deformity, and dubbed himself "King Richard" (after the royal hunchback), a nickname which his cronies usually shortened to "Dick."

"As to Lincoln," said Dick, "I won't yield to nobody in speakin' praise. He desarves it. Wise an brave 's the word when ye name *him*. He was a better man 'n Cæsar, though, to my thinkin'. But I shan't make no speech. I'll tell a story o' suthin' as took place in th' yarmy when Lincoln was my division commander. It's about a ghost, an' a hangin' match."

"What? did they hang a ghost?" asked Longshort, pricking up his ears.

"Ye'll know," replied Richard, "if ye'll listen. You see, we had one feller in our rigiment thet was 'bout one-half Tory an' t'other half scapegrace. He was in all kinds o' scrapes — continooally makin' trouble for himself an' the rest on us. I allers thought he was a Britisher in continentals. Well, he made several attempts to git away, and desart to the inimy. But he never succeeded. The last time he tried it he was detected an' fetcht up 'fore a court-martial. Gin'ral Lincoln was detarmined to make an example of him, to all th' yarmy, so he was tried, and sentenced to be hung instid o' shot. As he was on his way to the gallus the division surgeon happened to pass and see him. The surgeon took a good look at the doomed feller, an' arter speakin a word or tew to the rigimental surgeon on duty, he went off to his quarters. When we arriv' at the place o' execution, our rigiment was drawed up in a holler square, s'rroundin' a big tree. A sort o' ladder was set agin the tree, an' the crim'nal was walked up the ladder to whar the rope swung from a limb. Then they fastened the noose round the feller's neck. Wall, so fur, so good; but when they cum t' knock out the ladder from under, and the man dropped, his heft broke the rope, and down he fell, ker-thrash right ont' the ground!—I tell ye, it made us feel kinder sick all over to see that."

"Did they let him off, then?" asked Longshort.

"No. If 't had been his fust offence, p'raps they would, but he was too old a villain. So Left'nant Hamilton ordered another rope. And when one was brought, he tried with all his strength to break it, an' bein' as it held him, he concluded 't was a sure thing this time. They hitched the desarter to 't, an' sent him swingin' agin; but I'm bless'd 'f *that* rope didn't break, too. Ye see, it spun round wi' the weight, an' then it parted. So down cum the feller to the ground once more! As soon as we see that, we reckoned that man warn't born to be hung. We pitied the poor scamp, and we all begun to holler 'Mercy, mercy!' 'Let him go!' 'Pardon him!' 'That's enough!'

"So Major Ladson galloped off to headquarters, an' told Gin'ral Lincoln all about both failures, an' how the army cried for mercy on the scoundrel. Upon that, the gin'ral gin orders to spare him the third hangin', but he was to be drummed out o' camp, an' if ever afterwards he should be ketched inside the lines, he should die the shortest way. So we set the mis'able wretch on his legs (for he was more scairt 'n hurt), an' started him a-goin', an' the drummers beat the Rogue's March behind till he was out o' sight.

"Wall, about midnight, as the division surgeon was writin' in his quarters ('t was a barn jest outside o' camp), he heard somethin' creepin' kinder sly under the floor. He looked up — an' then I guess thar was *one* putty well astonished man in that barn. Thar was a figger risin' right up through a hole in the floor! It cum towards him, an' he could see the featurs; an' lo an' behold, 't was the very same man that he'd seen goin' to the gallus that mornin', an' thet he s'posed was dead an' buried. Wall, the old surgeon didn't know whether 't was flesh an' blood or a ghost; so says he:

"'Who are ye? Where d' ye cum from? What do ye want? Ain't you the feller 'twas hung this morning?'

"Now, ye see, the app'rition couldn't answer all them questions to once, so he begun by answe'in' the last one fust.

"'Yes, sir,' says he, in a thin, shaky voice, 'I'm the man you see a-goin to the gallus, an' I *was* hung, but ——'

"'Keep yer distance!' hollered the surgeon, who'd begun to feel streaked now, sure enough, tho' he was a brave man. The idee o' bein' visited at midnight by a character that was hung that mornin', warn't at all gratifyin' to him. He had every reason to s'pose 't was the ghost o' that executed crim'nal, an' nothin' more.

"'Keep your distance,' says he. 'Don't ye git any nearer to me till ye tell what ye cum for!'

"'I cum to beg suthin to eat,' says the feller, in a half whisper, "I ain't no ghost, doctor. The ROPE BROKE when they was a hangin' me, — it broke TWICE, doctor — an' then the rigiment got a pardon for me. I'm ordered not to cum back on pain o' death, but I resked it, for I was most starved, an' I thought you'd pity me.'

"When the surgeon heard that he laffed.

"'Oho!' said he. 'If that's the case, you may eat and welcome; but don't ye never appear so sudden agin to folks that b'leave ye dead.'"

"A pretty good ghost story," said Longshort, "and jist about as much real ghost in it as there is in any on 'em. But your telling o' that hangin' brings to my mind another 't I seed down South. There was tew lawless rapscallions amongst us that we couldn't dew nothin' with. They was slippery as Jack Sheppard, an' wicked as Cain, Judas Iscariot, and the twelve Cæsars, all rolled inter one. They was in for all kinds o' diviltry, whether 't paid or not; the army despised 'em, and the people hated 'em — an', to tell the trewth, *feared* 'em, tew. Wall, these 'ere villains was fin'lly took an' tried, an' condemned to be hung."

"Where was it?" asked Dick, the hunchback.

"'T was in Augusty, Georgy, an 't the very time, tew, when the place was besieged by the inimy. Waal, as I was sayin', they was both condemned to the gallus. But when a hangman was wanted, ther' couldn't a sojer in the lines be found that 'ud volunteer to play Jack Ketch to them tew reprobates. They was so all-fired bad, not a decent man 'ud tech 'em. Somehow, I dunno but the idee 'd got round thet they was in league with the Old Harry, an' so anybody 't handled 'em 'ud have a cuss follerin' him ever arterwards.

"Wall, when the off'cers found they couldn't git a hangman amongst the troops (an' they didn't like ter *force* us to 't, ye know), they concluded to pardon the least rascal o' the tew (an' 't was mighty hard to tell which), *provid d he'd hany t' other*. When the terms was proposed to the feller, he warn't none tew good t' accept 'em, an' save his own neck. So he went back on his old confed'rate, an' said he'd dew the job. Now, mind ye, the inimy was a-firin' on us all that time, from the batteries outside. Wall, the villain that was to dew the hangin' went to work, 'cordin' to orders, on the villain that was to be hung, an' in bloody quick time he'd sent him off on his long journey, with nothin' to walk on."

"He hung him, did he?" asked a fat man, who went by the name of Roundout, because his face was like a full moon.

"Yes, he hung him, and saved his own life. But he didn't keep it long. In a few minutes arterwards, an' whilst his comrade was danglin' from the rope, a cannon ball from one o 'the inimy's batteries struck him on the stomach, an' near 'bout cut him in tew!"

"I vum! One rascal foller'd t'other pretty close, didn't he?" commented Humpback.

"I should call that a raal judgment," said Roundout.

"Yes. Both on 'em was too wicked ter live, anyway. An' they'd sarved the divil in company so long, that they warn't 'lowed to break partnership."

"Here, poy," said one of the company, who looked as if he belonged to the ancient race of Knickerbockers, "hand me tat plate off apples, and ten you may hear a shtory apout a brafe lad tat I knew a goot many years ago."

The waiter, a smart little fellow of twelve or thirteen, promptly passed the plate, and Knickerbocker helped himself to a large, beautiful red apple. Taking out his knife, he cut the apple into halves, then, laying one hemisphere in the palm of his left hand, he fell to scraping off the pulp for his toothless mouth.

"You see, in '76, shoost after the Declaration off In-te-pendence, te Briteesh vas in dis citee, and tey shtaidt here a long vile. Te Americans had stationed demselves a few miles from 'ere, between te lines of te two armies. Very vell. Dere vas a fine garten, vich pelongdt to a vidow. Te produce off dis garten vent a goot vays to support te vidow. Put it vas often robbdt, and her most faluable tings carried off. Often tid she and her poy go out dere in de mornings, and find many tings shtolen, and oders all tramlet unter voot. Ten tey vould cry, and scholdt, and vish fader vas alife. 'He vould put a shtop to soosh doings!' tey said."

"*That* didn't dew no good," interrupted Longshort. "I never knowed scoldin' to stop thievin'. I'l tell ye what they oughter done; they oughter watched for the robber, and shot him in the act."

"You tink zo?" replied Knickerbocker, putting a mouthful of scooped apple on his tongue. "Vell, I tell you tey did something petter."

"What was that?" asked Humpback Dick.

"Vy, you see, te vidow's son vas a brafe leedle fellow. Zo he says: 'Moder, led me vatch for te tief. I'll take fader's gun and loadt it, and ven te tief comes, I'll make it shpeak to him.'

"Very vell; you see, te vidow at first tought her poy, only sixteen years oldt, could do noting to prevent te robbery, and might get himself shot; zo she von't led him go."

"That's jest the way," grumbled Longshort, interrupting again, " mothers make raal cowards o' their boys, keepin' 'em in so. She oughter let him watch, an' tried him."

"Yaw, tat's shoost vat she did do," said old Knickerbocker. "You vait, and led *me* talk. Very vell. Te poy teased his moder a vile, and ten she con-sented to led him vatch in te garden von night. She chargdt him and chargdt him how to behave, ven te robber should come, and he says: 'Moder, I must do as I can know best ven I see him.' And zo te leedle fellow gets his fader's gun down, and loads it. Ven night came he vent in te garden out, and hidt himself in a snug place, pehindt some trees. Very vell. I'y and py dere came sneaking into te yardt a great, strapping Highlandter, who pelongdt to te Brit-eesh Grenadiers. He filldt full a large pag in his hand slily mit peaches, and ten he turn to go avay. Shoost ten te poy comes tiptoe out, and thteal oop softly behindt mit his gun. 'You are my prisoner!' says he, sudden, making his voice as big round as he could. 'Go forwardt, ofer in sat roadt, or I shoots you deadt,' says he.

"Te Highlandter he joomped, for he vas took short oop mitout any varnin', and he knowdt notings who was after him. He didn't vant to pe shot, and zo he tought he'd petter do as te poy toldt him. He had his side-arms on, but tey vas no goot to him, for his handts was holding his bag, and te poy vouldn't led him trop it. Zo he got in te roadt ofer, mit te poy close behindt him, and if he stopped, or looked apout making any suspicious motions, the poy vould threaten to shoot. Zo they vent on all te vay, te leedle hero behindt, mit his gun cocked retty to fire off, and I tell you, he trove that pig, strapping grenadier into te American camp, and delifered him oop a prisoner off var!

"Ven te soldier had permission to trow his pag down, and look roundt, he felt awfu ashamed to see who his captor vas. He could have stivered tat poy mit one plow off his fist — if he had only known. Ach, but it vas too lade now — and all he could do vas to grumble. 'Hoot anaw,' says he, 'a Briteesh grenadier made prisoner by soosh a brat — soosh a *brat!*'"

"What did the American officers say?" inquired Humpback Dick.

"Say? Vy, tey said tat was a prafe and nople poy, and if they had an army of soosh poys, they could drive all te red-coats out of te landt."

"They oughter gin the young feller a reward," said Longshort, "he desarved it."

"Tat vas vat tey did. Tey made oop a collection off seferal poundts, and gafe to him, and te poy vent home proudt to his proudt moder."

By this time the old Dutch soldier had scraped his apple down to the shell, and he and the other veterans, finding that it was past nine o'clock, left the inn, and went to their homes.

THE END.

BOOK NOTICES.

THE AULD SCOTCH MITHER, AND OTHER POEMS. IN THE DIALECT OF BURNS. By J. E. RANKIN. ILLUSTRATED BY HERPICK AND OTHERS. BOSTON: D. LOTHROP & CO. 1873. 12mo. Pp. 125.

Most careful readers of the higher specimens of the better class of newspapers have seen occasional poems by Dr. Rankin circulating about, distinguished alike for the flexible accuracy with which they have reproduced the old Scotch dialect that Burns made at once popular and famous, and for the genuinely Christian domesticity which saturates them through and through. Some of them have been widely copied and strongly complimented, and they richly deserved the distinction. These, with not a few others that had never before come to the public eye, are here collected into a tasteful and well-illustrated volume, and are now sent forth on their pleasant and peculiar errand. It is a unique literary offering which they make up, redolent of the glens and hights, the brigs and lochs, the forest and heather, the castles of the by-gone time, and the pleasant homes of the present which are peculiar to Scotland. Not a few of the pieces have in them the sweetness of a musical rhythm and the sensibility of a brave and tender soul. None are feeble or commonplace, and some of them possess a merit, both in substance and form, that would be noticeable among the products of those whose songs have made melody for a continent. — Rev. Dr. Day in *Morning Star*.

LITTLE THREE-YEAR-OLD. By MRS. C. E. K. DAVIS. BOSTON: D. LOTHROP & CO., PUBLISHERS. 16mo. pp. 164. 75 c.

Mrs. Davis, in her sketches of little three-year-old Tina, has shown that she understands and sympathizes with childhood, knows its experiences and fancies, apprehends what is peculiar in its prose and its poetry, and can paint it with such a real life-likeness that it comes out from the covers of her book and stands forth a living, breathing, exhilarating thing. Belonging to the same department of literature as Sophie May's Dotty Dimple and Prudy Books, it is every way worthy to stand beside them on the shelf. It is a taking little book which she has wrought out, and she need not fear but that her readers will plead for more of the same sort. — *Methodist Home Journal*.

MYSTERY OF THE LODGE. By MARY DWINNELL CHELLIS, BOSTON: D. LOTHROP & CO. 1873. 12 mo. pp. 388.

A thoroughly good book. Miss Chellis never fails to write with vivacity and a high moral aim. She is effective even when failing to be artistic, and one feels the strong beating of a true heart. In the Mystery of the Lodge she seems chiefly aiming to set forth the superior value of a genial, sunny, sympathetic, helpful religion, over that which is dogmatic, formal, stern and cynical, -- to show how Christian love in the heart rises above systematic theology in the head. In bringing out this lesson she sketches for us a variety of interesting characters, and fills her narratives and colloquies with a zest and magnetism that forbid the reader to grow dull. — *Morning Star*.

BOOK NOTICES.

FAITHFUL BUT NOT FAMOUS. A Historical Tale. By the Author of "Soldier Fritz," &c Boston: D. LOTHROP & CO., Publishers. 1873. 16mo. pp. 305.

This volume gives a most interesting account of the origin and early progress of the Protestant Reformation in France. It carries us back three centuries, and sets us down in the very midst of the life prevailing at that early day both at the French capital and in the provinces. The real history has been followed, and most of the events recorded are such as are familiar to all careful readers of historical literature. More or less of the prominent personages of that period are dealt with, and the narratives and portraitures exhibit real skill. It is a species of literature that is every day gaining in prominence, and that does a very wholesome work. The book shows that fiction is not essential to a vital interest, that valuable knowledge may be given in a most entertaining form, and that the great struggles between good and evil that have shaken the world and that are still to go on till the truth becomes triumphant, may enlist the strongest sympathy of those who have yet to find and perform the most important part of their work in the world. Such books as this can hardly be multiplied too freely or be commended to the young in too emphatic a way —*Pastor and People.*

THE BLOUNT FAMILY. By Rev. THERON BROWN. D. LOTHROP & CO., Boston. Pp. 459. Illustrated. $1.50.

This is one of the "One Thousand Dollar Prize Series," and, in our judgment, is the best story that Mr. Brown has written. In style it is unusually discriminating and careful, and it abounds with scenes of domestic life, which are so striking, yet so true to human nature, so finely descriptive and so happily penned, that they seem to bring the reader into close companionship with the characters of the narrative. The two boys are traced along a checkered but significant career, from the early period when they lost their father, to early and noble manhood. But the story of the mother's devotion, and energy, and pluck, and womanly trust, is especially stimulating and valuable as a practical lesson. It is one of the few books that will repay a second reading.—*Youth's Companion.*

This is a good book. The difference between real religion and the superficial is clearly marked, and the power of the genuine strikingly illustrated. "An unaided woman makes a home for herself, and, actuated by the fear of God and the instincts of holy affection, is assured of being blessed and protected, and becomes the means of helping others onward and upward."

The story must awaken a new admiration for a mother's love, and strengthen that faith which is more than knowledge and the hope that outlives hardship and wrong. It is shown that piety and good sense will make the poor prosperous, the sweet excellencies of patience, self-denial, industry, cheerfulness and filial duty are illustrated, and reverence for justice, temperance, truth purity, and the Bible are inculcated.—*Christian Era*

OPINIONS EXPRESSED.

"A WHITE HAND. By Ella Farman. (D. Lothrop & Co.) This book is brightly and vivaciously written, and deals with the social problems of the present time, conservatively indeed, but with refreshing earnestness and delicacy. The tale is interesting. Those who hate Dr. Clarke, and believe that a woman is as good as a man, if not better, will be disgusted at the wife who, with the assistance of her friend spent the best years of her life in bringing herself up to the standard of taste of a husband, handsome, fickle, and fine, who had chosen her once of his own free-will, and then grown discontented with her afterward. But, at least she succeeded; and that is something — and the moral and intellectual gains she made, for his undeserving sake, enriched her own nature. Millicent's white hand was not afraid to touch sin, sometimes, and sorrow, often — but her womanhood was so pure, her purpose so unselfish, that no contact was base enough to soil its whiteness. It is, I believe, the first attempt of its author, in this direction; and it is certainly successful in the present, while it promises yet better things for the future." *New York Tribune.*

A WHITE HAND. A Story of *Noblesse Oblige.* By Ella Farman. Boston: D. Lothrop & Co. 12mo. $1.50.

Miss Farman has produced a genuine American novel, of great power; original in conception, and bold in execution. It opens with a series of Portraits, strikingly drawn; and the story unfolds naturally, but with an intense interest, exciting and fascinating the calmest reader. Careless critics may call it sensational, but, while some incidents border on the improbable, the aim of the book is noble, and the characters are consistent throughout. Millicent Challis is a woman of lofty type, governed by the maxim that high birth and breeding demand high character — she is true to the law under stress of great temptation; and the influence of her example purifies and ennobles associates of weaker stuff and lower aims. It is a good novel to read. Its high ideal will please the thoughtful, and its dramatic power will attract and impress those who care only for an exciting story.—*Dr. Lincoln, in The Contributor.*

OPINIONS EXPRESSED.

THE LIFE OF AMOS LAWRENCE. 370 pages, 12mo, Illustrated. Price, $1.50. *Boston:* D. LOTHROP & Co., *Publishers.*

"American biography has been immeasurably enriched by the publication of this excellent contribution." — *Niagara Democrat.*

"As a business man Mr. Lawrence was a pattern. The pure and elevated character of his moral sentiments, and his deep religious sympathies, were the foundation of his character and fortune. Notwithstanding his numerous charities, he died a millionaire." — *Boston Traveller.*

"A life of spotless integrity and unexampled benevolence was his, and his life and character should be studied by every young man." — *Bangor Journal.*

"He was one of nature's noblemen, who used and loved wealth principally for the good and happiness it enabled him to confer on his fellowmen. His liberality was boundless as the ocean, yet moved and regulated by principle." — *Richmond Dispatch.*

"The example of a man who regulated every action of his life by a sense of his responsibility to God. The book must do good wherever it goes." — *Boston Daily Advertiser.*

"This volume reveals a man of greater *moral* power than the most gifted statesman of the age, — power whose fruits will bless the world for ages to come. It gives us a view of the *interior* character of the highest style of man. The example it holds up before young men is more valuable than rubies." — *Christian Observer.*

"Commencing life poor, by persevering industry, probity of character, and prudent enterprise, he rose to wealth and distinction, and united with remarkable and successful business talents and pursuits, a life of benevolence and religion." — *Albany Argus.*

"We are thankful for the volume. It reveals a *charity*, noble and active, while the young merchant was still poor, a beautiful cluster of sister graces — and the constancy and magnitude of his contributions to the cause of humanity and piety." — *North American Review.*

BOOK NOTICES.

THE OLD STONE HOUSE. By ANNIE MARCH. Boston: D. LOTHROP & CO.

We've read this book with real pleasure: One of the "Thousand Dollar Prize Series," it abounds in sterling common sense, sound principles, and a pure, practical piety. It has a healthy fragrance about it from first to last. True to Nature, it has a Spring-like freshness and vivacity, you find in it buds, blossoms, bird-song, sunshine, and merry life. At the same time it has, in parts, a dash of Autumn; just enough to make it sweetly pensive. The vernal and the autumnal gracefully meet and mingle. If the story, so true and so tender, never rises to the loftiest heights, it never sinks to a dead and dreary level. A grand nature is that of old "Aunt Faith," putting her life into the noble and self-denying service of rearing up for this life and the next, five orphan nieces and nephews. The book has *virtue* in it.—*Christian Era.*

FINISHED OR NOT. By the author of "Fabrics." Boston: D. LOTHROP & CO., Publishers. 1873. 12mo. pp. 360.

Finished or Not is every way worthy of the author, who has heretofore given ample proof of exceptional ability in dealing in an entertaining and popular way with some of the deeper problems of life. We have her thoughts on great themes embodied in the form of a story, and sh sets forth the qualities that she would exalt in a gallery of portraits. She is never feeble, never superficial, never heedless, never doubtful in her moral teaching; but her calm and thoughtful strength often comes out so that it sparkles, and stirs, and magnetizes, and lifts the reader as into a higher realm of life. For thoughtful, reflective and appreciative young people, the book will have a special charm and a large value.—*Watchman and Reflector.*

WILL PHILLIPS; OR, UPS AND DOWNS IN CHRISTIAN BOY-LIFE. Pp. 363. D. LOTHROP & CO., Publishers.

Will Phillips is a book especially meant for wide-awake boys. It shows that the author understands them, sympathizes with them, has a high appreciation of their best qualities, and a generous side for their excesses and faults. It is a fine exhibition of life at a large school for boys, setting forth the wholesome stimulants and the strong and subtle temptations met in such a sphere, and especially showing how a Christian character and life may be there maintained in connection with an earnest, generous, gleeful, boyish enthusiasm,— how an Academy pupil may be voted "a real good fellow" without a dissenting voice by the most audacious and jolly of his companions, and at the same time be so thoroughly true to the Great Master as to make every one confess the presence and power of the godly element. The book is thoroughly wholesome, it is written with ability and skill, and its vital interest is maintained even to the closing paragraph. — *Boston Daily Journal.*

An Original and Intensely Interesting Story of American Society. By the New and Brilliant Author, ELLA FARMAN.

A WHITE HAND.
PRICE $1.50.

"It will correct false standards of feeling, and warn many a warm heart of the danger that lies in 'just a friendship.'" — *Transcript.*

"The style is pure and elevated, the story original, of absorbing interest, and every way good." — *Interior.*

"Millicent is a rare character; pure and strong herself, she stooped and lifted up the weak, and inspired them with her own noble purposes." — *Baptist Union.*

"It is cheerful and pathetic, forcibly written, and of stirring interest." — *Daily Leader.*

"The heroine is a woman of lofty type, true to the law under stress of temptation; and the influence of her example purifies and ennobles associates of weaker stuff and lower aims." — *Washington County Post.*

"This book is brightly and vivaciously written, and deals with the social problems of the present time, conservatively, indeed, but with refreshing earnestness and delicacy." — *New York Tribune.*

"Its high ideal will please the thoughtful, and its dramatic power will attract and impress those who care only for an exciting story." — *Dr. Lincoln in the Contributor.*

"Millicent's white hand was not afraid to touch sin, sometimes — and sorrow, often — but her womanhood was so pure, her purpose so unselfish, that no conduct was base enough to soil its whiteness." — *Louise Chandler Moulton in New York Tribune.*

www.ingramcontent.com/pod-product-compliance
Lightning Source LLC
Chambersburg PA
CBHW022044230426
43672CB00008B/1064